Producing a play

Peter Chilver

B T Batsford Limited *London and Sydney*

© Peter Chilver 1974
First published 1974
ISBN 0 7134 2888 0
ISBN 0 7134 2876 7

Filmset by Tradespools Limited, Frome, Somerset
Printed in Great Britain by
The Anchor Press Limited, Tiptree, Essex
Bound by William Brendon and Son Limited, Tiptree, Essex
for the publishers
B T Batsford Limited
4 Fitzhardinge Street, London W1H 0AH
23 Cross Street Brookvale N S W 2100 Australia

Contents

Foreword

This book offers an introduction to some of the many skills involved in the production and staging of plays: directing and acting; staging, including the thinking out of improvised stages where existing facilities are inadequate or non-existent; designing, lighting and building scenery; and the working out of improvised productions.

No attempt is made to dogmatise, or to suggest that reading what somebody else has written is a substitute for doing the thing oneself, and for looking sympathetically at the work being done by others, both professional and amateur. Rather, a variety of suggestions are made, and it is hoped that the reader will be inspired to experiment with these for himself in a practical context.

The book is intended for anyone who is keen to consider the possibilities of theatre, perhaps as an absolute beginner, perhaps as someone who has much experience in one aspect of theatre craft and is interested to look at others.

Throughout the book I am drawing upon experience that is personal and varied. Since I make many specific references to it, it may be useful briefly to outline that experience: as a theatregoer, as a student-actor at drama school and (for a while) in the professional theatre, and as a teacher and lecturer in schools and colleges, directing and sometimes devising and writing shows for young people and students.

As a theatregoer mainly in London, and occasionally in Paris and New York, I have seen the work of many great actors, designers, directors, singers and dancers. I have also seen a great deal of excellent experimental theatre come (and alas go, in most cases) in places as disparate as the suburbs of Toronto, the parks of Vancouver and the pubs of London. Some of this experimental work has been created by professional groups, but the bulk of it has come from schools and colleges and independent amateur societies.

I have also had the good fortune to be involved in varying capacities in 'making' theatre myself. I have only briefly been a professional, but for a long time I have been paid to make theatre in schools and colleges. So that without ever becoming rich or famous, I have spent a great portion of my working life gainfully and cheerfully employed in one way or another in the business of theatre. My work as a teacher in schools has led me into directing plays for youth groups, devising productions specially for particular groups, and helping to form youth theatres. And my work with students at colleges of technology and, later, at a college for the training of teachers, has given me further chances to create theatre with people of widely differing backgrounds, ages and abilities. Before this, my life as an acting student and then as an actor allowed me to work alongside a large number of professionals, some of them distinguished, and almost all of them remarkably gifted. It also allowed me to work under a large number of equally gifted teachers and directors.

Perhaps the main conclusion which I would offer from this experience is that there seems to me to be a great abundance of talent which can be used to create excellent theatre, and that this abundance is everywhere. I have never yet worked among any group of people, young or old, amateur or professional, experienced or inexperienced, where there is a shortage of potentially useful actors, designers, singers and the like. But what is often lacking is the painstaking and detailed carefulness on the part of the director, the stage manager and the rest of the company (but especially the director as the 'captain' of the team) with which to put these talents together into an artistic piece of theatre. This, as Jean-Louis Barrault has suggested, is the only valid use of the term 'total theatre': the total commitment of all its participants to the total success of the production.[1]

Quite often the incompleteness of a production, its shoddiness or carelessness, emanates from an ignorance of what the rest of the team are doing and the problems they meet in trying to do it, not necessarily from an ignorance of one's own particular contribution. Yet the theatre is a collective art, and everyone is so inter-dependent on everyone else that we can only work and succeed *together*, not on our own. Gordon Craig said it all very clearly at the beginning of the century:

'Acting, scene, costume, lighting, carpentry, singing, dancing . . . no advance can come from fitful reform, but only from a systematic progression.'[2]

And seventy years later Peter Brook wrote:

'(Productions) most of the time are betrayed by a lack of elementary skills. The techniques of staging, designing, speaking, walking across a stage, sitting, even listening, just aren't sufficiently known.'[3]

Terms such as 'amateur', 'professional', 'West End' are often used to imply an inevitable order of excellence, but in fact all kinds of theatre — amateur or professional, musical or straight, classical or experimental, politically commited or simply frivolous — are capable of exciting their audience and also of boring them to death (and thereby discouraging them from coming again to *any* kind of theatre). And I suspect that when the latter happens it is the result not so much of a lack of inspiration as of a lack of conscientiousness — an inability to attend to, to begin to learn about, the basic skills out of which, as Craig and Brook indicate, all real theatre can grow.

1 The Idea of the Production

All productions emanate from some simple, basic idea. No matter how complex and varied the final piece of work may appear to be when it is presented to the audience, in its conception it is no more than a thought, an image, in one person's mind. 'How marvellous to do *The Cenci!*' or 'Why not dramatise the schoolchildren's strike of 1908!' or 'Could we get Albert Finney to do a musical version of . . .?' And whether we happen to be Bernard Delfont, who must then persuade his fellow board members, or the student who must then persuade his college drama society, we are all caught up in the same basic process: we must gain the support of a large number of other people to help us translate our idea into action. This is indeed the whole complexity of a production: we are so much in need of each other. Noël Coward apparently wrote some of his best plays in about three days. But it takes even the most professional of companies at least three weeks (at a modest estimate) to evolve a successful production of any of them.

And so, since the journey from idea to production is such a long one, and so highly social, involving us in sharing our skills, our enthusiasms, and our lives even, with so many other people, it may be useful to talk about this early stage when the idea is still just that: an idea. And one can begin by working backwards, so to speak, from some actual productions, some good, some bad.

Some productions revisited

One of the first productions I ever saw was a school rendering of *King Lear* in the late 1940s. Our English teacher responded to an invitation from a distant grammar school, hired a coach, and took forty or so thirteen-year olds to a somewhat forbidding town hall in a London suburb, where we witnessed a somewhat forbidding production of this somewhat forbidding play. Afterwards, on the way home, he apologised good naturedly for wasting our time, but he did not need to do so: we had laughed uproariously through most of the evening, and continued to laugh on the way home, and indeed carried on laughing for many days, weeks and even years afterwards, as we narrated the calamities of the production to those who did not have the good fortune to see it for themselves. The only incident that marred the happiness of the occasion was a letter from the headmaster of the school we visited complaining at our bad behaviour — which brings us neatly to the whole question of the audience's responsibility and the company's responsibility, and so to the very ethics of the theatre.

To the question, what went wrong with that now remote and otherwise forgotten production of *King Lear*, one can only answer — everything. To begin with, the school had hired a hall with which, quite obviously, neither the director nor his actors had the remotest acquaintance. It posed problems of acoustics of which they were blissfully unaware. It also presented visual problems, for the sight-lines were such that whole areas of the stage were invisible to vast sections of the audience. Not only that, but the play itself presented questions of a technical, as well as a psychological and a philosophical kind, with which no one appeared in any way to have wrestled.

The curtain opened late, roughly thirty minutes late, and then was closed again immediately to allow all the appropriate actors to assume their appropriate positions. Within minutes of its re-opening it was clear that no one would be able to hear a single word of the dialogue, but that we were all going to hear a great deal from the small orchestra (drums, trumpet and percussion) which was placed strategically and prominently in the small pit just in front of the stage. Deprived of any chance to hear what was happening, we could concentrate on the things we could see: an array of young actors dressed up in a great variety of vaguely medieval costumes which made them look unhappy, uncomfortable and unreal. Occasional scenic offerings were also placed before us. Prior to one particular battle scene the proscenium curtain was closed and the orchestra launched into a great fanfare of military preparation. Then, having concluded its piece, it rested. Nothing happened. Quite rightly, the orchestra filled the void with a repeat of the fanfare: drumroll, trumpet voluntary and clashing of cymbals. Still nothing happened. The curtain remained firmly closed. To the delight of the audience, the orchestra played the fanfare a third time, and now the curtain did actually open, to reveal a stage as empty as before but for the addition of two rather small tents, in front of which stood two soldiers. After an extremely long and inactive silence, the curtains closed again. The orchestra, indefatigable and British to boot, played the fanfare a fourth time. After this, it was quite clear that no matter what might or might not happen next, they would not play the fanfare again, despite one or two friendly suggestions from the audience that they should do so. Then, at last, the curtain opened again, and this time there were three small tents, not just two, and out of one of them came the leading actors, and the play, or rather the mime-play, continued.

Equally bad was a production I saw on Broadway many years later of the musical play *Mame*. Not that this was handicapped by any kind of obvious incompetence, and indeed the only successful sequence in the production was one which guyed the kind of classic theatrical incompetence which I have just been describing.

The production was graced by a few good songs, an attractively simple stage set which made good use of the height and width of the stage, and a good chorus. Technically everything was fine. Everybody came on and went off at the right time. The interval was not too long. And we could hear all the actors, for they used microphones which were working efficiently. But at the time I saw the production the original star, Angela Lansbury, had left the cast, and so I saw one of her several successors. The show no longer worked. Where Miss Lansbury had almost certainly brought a wit and a stylishness around which the production had been moulded, and upon which it must have depended very heavily, there was no longer anything bold or clear enough for the audience to hold on to. The script was littered with fairly obvious jokes, and the company built up to them with well-drilled efficiency. This is it! Joke coming! This is where you laugh. But nothing happened. Throughout the entire evening. Two complete acts without action. A drama without life.

Before moving on to better things, let me cite briefly a production in Paris of the Tennessee Williams play *Sweet Bird of Youth*, with the celebrated Edwige Feuillère in the central role of the American film star who suddenly comes face to face with the passing of youth, of career and of life itself. It is a difficult and interesting play, in which the audience must be absolutely convinced of the megalomania and the sexuality of the star, alongside the decadence and sheer brutality of Williams' Deep South, which provides both the setting and the immediate reason for the tragedy. But in this particular production we could have been anywhere. The sets were vague, neither this period nor that, neither this sector of society nor that, and failed to compensate for this with any real or appropriate atmosphere. Geographically, socially and psychologically we were in no particular place at all. And this was mirrored in the acting itself.

Nobody on stage ever appeared actually to meet anybody else. The two lovers in the long opening scene appeared to be virtually oblivious of one another. Feuillère was magnificent from time to time: in her great tirades, which are virtually monologues, she pulled us to her out of the auditorium and caught us up in her drama. Then, as other characters intruded, the play lapsed again. All the pieces of the machine, as it were, arrived at the right place at the right time, but never interlocked.

And what about some successes? I remember, for instance, a school production of *Treasure Island* where the director turned the unwieldy school hall first into Bristol harbour, then into a vast ship and then into an island. The audience sat on both sides facing inwards, and the stage at one end and the doors at the other provided the actors with their exits and entrances. There were fourteen spotlights, two floodlights, two large double-ladders, a few hired costumes and many improvised ones, forty actors and a couple of small units of scenery which the actors carried on and off. And the effect was total theatre: the audience was completely engaged from start to finish. Why?

Amateur productions that are good possibly benefit from the many that are bad; the good ones seem, by sheer contrast, to be very good. In the professional theatre the situation can be dangerously the reverse: because we have paid more and travelled a greater distance and heard so much about it, we may lack the patience to settle down and give the production time. In other words we may demand a kind of instant spectacle which the production may quite rightly be unable to offer us. I suspect that it is for this reason, among others, that I have often been more moved by productions of straight plays outside the West End than inside. There is less fuss in going, and so I can offer my relaxed attention.

More important, though, with *Treasure Island* was the novelty of the staging and the panache with which the players sketched in the characters they were playing. And more important still was the overall conception of the production. It was as if the director and the company were saying to us: life can be fun, amusing, a romp, an adventure, or at least a part of it can be, as we are showing you this evening. And the athleticism and youthfulness of the cast, and the agility of the improvised ways in which the director and designer created the stage and the settings, perfectly expressed this philosophy. And this in its turn was complemented and turned into theatre by the sheer efficiency of all the production team, stage management and front-of-house included.

And this brings us back to a basic point: a production will succeed as a whole because of the rightness of *every* single part, and similarly fail as a whole because of the wrongness of *any* single part. We often tend to be critical of the kind of person who comes out of the theatre saying simply, 'I liked it' or 'I didn't like it,' but the appropriateness of such a comment cannot be improved upon. For a production works either entirely or not at all. The refinements of criticism are good, they help us to understand more of the piece of theatre we have just been watching, and also help the director and company to understand something of what went wrong, but they remain expressions of a basically frustrating experience: that of watching and listening and yet failing to respond. And so the performance of one individual actor may to some extent compensate us for the evening's failure (and we end up concentrating on his skill, his costume, his contribution to the production) but the evening remains a failure for all that. As a work of art, any piece of theatre operates on an all or nothing basis.

It also operates on a here and now basis. Productions are not simply transferable. *Treasure Island*, for example, worked well the time I saw it, but how would it have translated to a conventional theatre? How well would the actors have coped with a run of say, a hundred performances? How would it have survived the scrutiny of quite different audiences – or the loss of any of the leading players and their replacement by understudies – always presuming that understudies were actually rehearsed and available? I mention such points merely in order to underline the extraordinarily fragile nature of any theatrical success, and especially to underline the significance of the specific players, specific theatre and specific audience to the success of a production, and thus to its initial idea and conception.

A useful illustration of this was the original London production of *West Side Story* which I saw six times, and which each time offered me in some way a different and exciting experience. But by the time of my sixth visit the greater proportion of the original cast had returned to America and had been replaced by British performers. The production no longer worked. Its whole force and impact had evaporated. Why? Because the new actors were not good enough? I suggest not. Rather, it was a matter of placing actors into an existing production, instead of creating a new one around them and their talents, just as the production originally had been created around the talents of the first cast. Similarly a very long run of a production can succeed in killing itself off; the actors may no longer bring to the show the particular skills at their command, and they need producing anew.

Among works that have deeply moved me, I would include a production of Ibsen's *John Gabriel Borkman* at the Royal

Academy of Dramatic Art in the early 1960s. It was directed by a student (Richard Digby Day) with a student cast. It had extreme simplicity and austerity; no money had been made available and so there was no scenery: the small stage was open and empty but for a bench or two. The company worked well together, and the actors took their time. We knew within moments of the opening that we would have to listen carefully and patiently: we must be in no hurry. And the director had rightly judged not only his theatre and his company, and how to use both, but also his audience. We were all fellow students of drama, and there were not many of us (because of the smallness of the theatre). We unconsciously knew the kind of adjustments which would be expected of us, including the basic fact that the leading actor would be many years too young for the role he was playing.

At about the same time that I saw the production of *Borkman*, I myself produced a musical play in the same theatre at RADA, again as a freelance student venture. It involved a company of about twenty students, and the show was written and composed and directed by myself, and it was a complete calamity. One of the teachers had the goodness of heart to say several encouraging things about it, but everybody else loathed it, and in the end so did I. Where did it go wrong?

It was very much the work of a beginner — my first production, my first written play — but subsequent experience in writing and directing makes me believe that its weakness lay elsewhere, and that the show's failure emanated from its principal virtue, which was its austerity. In order to get the show on to the stage, without money and without any facilities other than the use of the stage itself, I cut down ruthlessly on every possible accessory: no extra instrumentalists (one paid pianist); no changes of lighting (because no time to rehearse a lighting plot or fix it up); and no changes of costume. But the austerity which worked so brilliantly *for* the production of the Ibsen play, worked entirely *against* my musical. It needed all kinds of visual variety which I failed to give. More seriously, I also created the script in a void, and then led myself to believe that I had found the actors for it from among my class-mates at drama school. I would have done much better to work the other way round: to look sympathetically at the talents of my friends and start creating the show from that point on. Of course, none of this would have mattered if I had been a genius, either as writer or director. But I was not. I was not even a competent craftsman. So I ended up with a production in which I could myself have played all the parts and in which none of the actual actors was shown to advantage, and in a theatre which was quite wrong for the production itself. And its sole justification was that it taught me a lot which only became apparent when, quite a bit later, I tried to write and to direct again.

Among my other souvenir-calamities, I should also mention a quite good production which I once mounted in the round, and which failed utterly and irredeemably because in lighting the actors we also happened to blind the audience. We had not thought at all about the possibility of the light falling on to the audience, but it did, most efficiently. We had been unable to hang the lamps from the ceiling immediately above the stage area, and had hung them instead from the walls opposite. And the height of the walls was insufficient. As a result the audience spent the entire performance shielding their eyes with their hands, and that was the end of the production. We could have foreseen this. But we did not.

In all these various productions that I have mentioned, the weakness or the virtue lay in the very conception of the shows. It was not a matter of something going unpredictably or fortuitously wrong at the last minute.

If we take the school production of *King Lear*, this was unrelated at the very start to the skills and talents of the players, and to the demands of the theatre in which it was to be staged. It was conceived in a limbo which had no point of contact with reality.

The production of *Mame* was clearly conceived as a vehicle for a great star, not necessarily or exclusively for the one star who first created the role, but for a number of possible stars like her, who can invest quite ordinary material with great wit and glamour. And at the time I saw it, the production desperately needed rethinking and reworking for the particular actress who had taken over the part.

With *Sweet Bird of Youth* the error lay in the assumption that a production of that particular play could succeed purely on the strength of a great leading lady acting more or less on her own, whereas the play needed a real 'company' production. And it failed because it did not get it.

Treasure Island and *John Gabriel Borkman* both worked because the directors had created something which, as an idea, had taken into account the limitations and talents of their particular companies and theatres. *West Side Story* is perhaps more complex, in that one can imagine the basic idea going through numerous metamorphoses, dictated by both business and art, before Jerome Robbins finally staged it. But even here that basic idea is right: a great choreographer creating from the text of music, lyrics and book (all of them brilliant) and working with a gifted company of dancers, all of whom could act, and some of whom could sing, a piece of theatre in which acting, singing and dancing would assume equal significance.

And, of course, my venture 'in the round' failed because I had not said to myself from the start: this must be lit; can we do it? And if so, exactly how?

To place a production such as Jerome Robbins' *West Side Story* alongside a school drama production may seem odd to some people. But any work of art stands or falls by its impact upon the audience. And the audience can be as deeply affected by a production by inexperienced amateurs as one by highly gifted professionals. Any two companies will not be able to do the same thing equally well: they will have aptitudes for different things. And the excellence of the conception of an idea for a production will depend on the ability to see this. It is not a question of audiences lowering their standards as they move down the hierarchy of theatres. To do so is not only to kill off one's own response, but is also unfair to the actors themselves. In general actors do not say to themselves, 'This is not Shaftesbury Avenue or Broadway, so I'll hold back tonight.' They do their best. The place is immaterial to their commitment.

This brings us back to the headmaster who complained of the audience's behaviour at the performance of *King Lear*. But how then, was such an audience or the actors themselves ever to learn that *Lear* was other than a strange farce, or that there was more to theatre than learning lines and dressing up, other than through a full and spontaneous response to what was happening on the stage? No doubt the headmaster would reply that his school drama society was not the Old Vic, and that we in the audience should have been trained to make allowances for that fact. But should we? Why do *King Lear* if you cannot do it, and if there are so many other things that *can* be done? Or are we supposed to bring to theatre the kind of half-hearted attention that we bring so much of the time to radio and television, where we half attend while doing something else? But then the theatre has the added disadvantage that we cannot do anything else while we are actually sitting there.

We must always have the right to expect the best. And indeed the endless mystery of theatre is that the best will come unpredictably. We are constantly surprised. We may reasonably form all manner of expectations about the way a talent grows and matures, but the sudden emergence of untried talent of great skill and sophistication makes a kind of nonsense of all this. The London stage has recently offered two instances of young talent displaying great technical skill and accomplishment. The young girl who first played Baby June in the London production of *Gypsy* performed with wit and precision, and handled the enthusiasm of her audiences with all the panache of an experienced professional. In a very different way, Peter Firth's performance as the boy in *Equus* at the National Theatre had a depth and power which again belied his years. This is not to deny that such performances were the product of anything less than hard work from the performers and from those they worked with. It does serve, though, to remind us that the theatre can thrive on a great variety of very different kinds of talent, and that such talent can itself only thrive if given the opportunity. The latter may seem a rather obvious point but it is also the most important. There is an enormous amount of talent around. And the very idea of a production needs to be based on an awareness of the talent that is there. This is what we have. What can we make with it?

So the idea of a production is rooted in four related questions:

1 What kind of company? What skills do we already possess? What experience do we have? Are we used to working together? Do we have a variety of personnel to do all the various tasks that a production entails? Or do we have the people who are willing to learn such tasks, and others who will teach them?

Nor will this come down to the simple question, are we amateur or professional? In fact the opportunities facing a well-organised amateur company are in certain ways greater than those facing the professional. Facilities are often better; increasingly so in schools and colleges, though the most terrible facilities still prevail here and there. And since salaries do not have to be paid, large casts can be involved; more and more in the professional theatre, casts have to be small (outside of the large state-subsidised companies and the big musicals). We are told that managements will seldom touch a new play with a cast of more than seven or eight. So what a splendid opportunity for the amateur companies to encourage new talent among writers of epics, extravaganzas and plays with large casts!

So, in working out the idea of a production, we look closely at the people we have. If they are young, can any of them play older characters? What kind of characters, what kind of style, are within their reach? What are the variations in talent — in age and aptitude? Do we have gymnasts and athletes, singers, dancers?

When highly experienced actors are brought together and given the chance to work as a company for a long period of time, then the most complex and sophisticated theatre is possible. When government subsidy allows such a group to materialise (or private subsidy, as with Sir Barry Jackson's Birmingham Repertory Theatre) then audiences can travel miles and spend small fortunes in the reasonably sure conviction that what they see will be well worth the trouble. Sometimes, inevitably, they will be disappointed, but in general the productions of such companies will be beacons to everyone who believes in the theatre: audiences, actors, amateurs, professionals. But they will not eclipse or replace the work of everyone else. There will always be a need for all kinds of theatre and all kinds of companies. More theatres create more audiences, more actors, more writers . . . in short, they create more opportunities for the creative talent.

2 What kind of theatre?   This means literally, what kind of stage do we have, and within what kind of auditorium? Do we have a ready-made theatre? If so, is it right as it is for a particular production? Or must it be adapted and improvised to render it more flexible? Or do we have to create a stage where there is none at all? And what are the means at our disposal for helping us to answer all these questions — what equipment do we have — what building skills? All these factors enormously affect the very idea of a production. Likewise, what facilities do we have backstage? What are the acoustics of the auditorium? One may add that it is very difficult to transplant a production designed for one kind of stage on to a different stage altogether. When the recent Royal Shakespeare Company production of *Antony and Cleopatra* made the journey from Stratford to London, the stage designs did not quite fit on to the new stage. A fair amount of the action was no longer visible to the entire audience.

3 What kind of production?   There are many different kinds of theatre (using the word now in a more philosophical context) and the tendency to be snobbish about any of them seems to me a mistake. Straight plays; revue; musical; ballet; opera; extravaganzas; music hall; documentaries; improvised productions; and then, of course, all the different classifications of a straight play into farce, light comedy, thriller and the like. They all have their validity, for they all find a responsive audience. And all forms of theatre clearly benefit from an acquaintance with other forms. For instance, the plays of Alan Bennett and of Peter Nichols, who are two of the finest modern playwrights, clearly find their inspiration in part from theatre that lies outside their own genre, from music hall and revue in particular.

In the earliest stages of working out our ideas for a production, it may well be worth while considering possibilities under all of these headings. Stanislavsky, for instance, was much in favour of music hall as a way of training the inexperienced actor to project both the voice and the characterisation.

4 What kind of audience? One of the popular caricatures of the theatrical impresario is of an obviously rich gentleman with little sense of, or feeling for, art or artists, and a great affection for money. Part and parcel of the same view of 'the man behind it all', is a somewhat contemptuous view of the audience: that they want the vulgar (whatever that may mean!) and the poor. 'They don't want, and they can't appreciate the best!' Sometimes this cynicism takes the form of an attempted classification of audiences: bourgeois, mass, middle class, typically Home Counties, and so on. And always with the absolute conviction that the speaker or writer is not himself a member of these amorphous groups, and that such audiences are inferior to his own artistic standards.

No doubt such generalisations, and the prejudices they reveal, are best understood as part of the enthusiasm with which the reformer seeks to reform the theatre of his time. But I suspect that they do a great disservice also. First, in asserting that a particular kind of theatre is for *them* rather than *us*, we automatically imply that our theatre is for us rather than them: we make the theatre more, not less, elitist. Secondly, all dogmatising about the kind of audience one wants or does not want inevitably involves us in dogmatising about the kind of theatre one is aiming to create. And in the end this kills off talent more than it creates it. Indeed, the more we know about the psychology (and sociology) of the creative talent (and we still know remarkably little, and probably always will) the clearer it is that freedom, and the chance therefore to experiment, is the essential condition for creativity. In this way, any 'school', or 'method', must be careful that it does not stifle the very commodity which it presumably holds most dear.

Popular laments about the kinds of theatre which do actually flourish often seem to me equally ill-judged. The aim is not to demolish what is already there, but to add to it; not to stop people seeing light comedies, but to let more people see them, and to let more people see all other kinds of theatre also.

An illustration of the success of the non-dogmatic approach to artistic and theatrical growth is to be found in the career of the Royal Ballet Company, from its earliest days as the brainchild of Ninette de Valois, down to its present size and grandeur. In her conception of what ballet is and can be, de Valois has clearly been courageously bold and experimental and open-minded. Hence the growth of a classical tradition alongside excellent new choreography from artists as strongly different in their philosophy of the dance as John Cranko, Kenneth Macmillan and Frederick Ashton. A ballet as unusual and powerful as Ashton's *Enigma Variations* can only be created in an atmosphere uncluttered with dogma, and amidst a company where people know each other and have worked a great deal together.

In particular, de Valois did not believe that the audience for ballet was as restricted or exclusive as theatre history up till her time in England would seem to indicate. Nor did she believe, despite what she was probably told many times, that English audiences would only patronise ballet companies from abroad; even though, again, there would have been fair historical evidence for just such a belief. As a result, she was able to employ her energy, her resilience, her organising powers and her creative talents to achieve the miraculous: to turn an idea into an institution, into something with an existence entirely of its own.

I suggest, too, that the different opportunities for different kinds of theatre are so great that there is always the chance to do something everywhere. There need never be a vacuum. Even where we cannot do the thing we would most like to do, or imagine we would most like, we can still do something valuable. There is always need for experiment and improvisation, for pub theatres, street theatres, theatres of psychotherapy, music halls, and for all manner of new departures and also all manner of representations of the old and the familiar. Nor do I believe that these different kinds of theatre depend on exclusively different kinds of audience. They express different kinds of experience to which all of us can respond at various times.

We could put it this way: there is always an audience for good theatre, even though it will often be very, very difficult to find it! Gordon Craig sums it up neatly:

'It is utterly impossible to believe that the failure of the theatre today is due to a low standard of public taste. Public taste was never better than it is going to be tomorrow.' [4]

2 The Director

Learning to direct

Schools for actors exist in great abundance. Schools for directors hardly exist at all, apart from a few courses in some American universities which are part of a wider programme in 'theatre arts'. Then how does one learn to direct? Presumably by taking part in other people's productions, by looking at other productions and by doing one's own productions. And it is under these three headings that I would like to look at the work of the director, with the focus the same in each case: what skills are involved?

1 The director as actor   My first experience of being directed as an actor was in a college production at Oxford of Ben Jonson's *Epicoene, or the Silent Woman*. We rehearsed over a period of eight weeks, three or four times a week, two hours or so at a time. The director was Michael Baldwin. We staged it in a small hall on a small stage, with curtains for scenery, a few props and barely adequate lighting. The play itself is a difficult one: the plot twists and turns through numerous involutions, the language is complex, and the characters unattractive and exaggerated. Early in rehearsals a leading actor had to withdraw, and I took over his part: that of Morose, a miserable old bachelor who (a) is worth a fortune and (b) cannot abide the sound of any voice except his own. These two factors provide the pivotal points of the drama.

The production was a good one: funny and lively and grotesque. How was it done?

There was virtually no discussion that I can recall about the kind of play we were doing, nor about the historical period, nor about the reasons why any of the characters behaved in the particular ways they did. We were told to learn our lines immediately, and we were given the moves at the first rehearsals with which we stayed throughout. We were often invited to overdo our actions, to make them abundantly clear to the audience. And my script from that production bears the notes pencilled into the margin: 'boldly', 'meanly', 'viciously', 'tragically wounded'. It seems in fact that I was finally playing one character with four main sub-characters within him, who were arrogant, selfish, vulnerable and suspicious in turn. But this was not at any point agreed on in so many words. It grew out of the attempts we made at rehearsal to make vivid sense in the action of the text itself.

The production made much business with fruit. Many of the characters were frequently eating, and at various points fruit was not only consumed but also thrown about! This helped to under-line the play's preoccupation with sexuality and fertility, and also gave the characters a modest amount of real business to attend to. And on a stage where we were unable to bring much in the way of furniture or props, it was vitally necessary to have something in the way of basic living to do, and not merely to have vast speeches to articulate; especially since Jonson was out to demonstrate that for all our verbosity and learning we were all extremely earthy, sensual, greedy and selfish beings.

We were also encouraged to work things out on our own and to bring back the results to show the rest of the company at rehearsal. I found immense difficulty, not surprisingly, with an enormous monologue in which Morose progresses from melan-cholia to virtual hysteria when he finds, or thinks he has found, an absolutely silent woman with whom he can spend the rest of his life. I was told to break the speech down into its com-ponent parts, and to make each part vivid to the audience. When I was unable to do this, I was told that the speech would have to be cut. I worked overtime to avoid this and found a way of making it right for myself, of making sense of the psychology of what was happening, and of conveying this in performance. In other words, on that particular occasion, within that particular production, I dared to experiment and to continue doing so until it seemed to work.

The business of experimenting, as actor or director, brings us to an important distinction between the professional and the amateur, and one where the amateur has in most instances a possible advantage. Because he has not committed his entire life and livelihood to the theatre, the amateur, whether student in college, or what you will, can more easily afford to take risks. The professional will often have too much to lose. And this can express itself not only in the established star who declines to do anything other than the light comedies in which he has made his name, but also in the insecurity of the young drama student at the acting academy. This is for many the awful surprise of going from school or college or amateur society to the professional drama school. What was previously such delight, such adven-ture, suddenly becomes daunting and serious and extremely difficult. This was certainly my own experience when I went to

RADA in the early 1960s. And indeed the Principal, John Fernald, spelt out this feeling very clearly for us when he first addressed the term's newcomers. He told us that we would feel for the first year as if we were being 'taken apart', that we would be made to rethink much that we had so far taken for granted about our talents and our personalities, and only much later would we feel we were coming together again. His prediction proved entirely accurate, at least as far as I was concerned, and it is certainly true that I never approached any of my work at RADA with the kind of confident sense of adventure with which I approached the production of *Epicoene* as a student (but not a drama student) at Oxford not so many years before.

Each term at RADA we were involved in two different productions, each time with different directors. (In addition we had the usual classes in speech, movement, fencing, etc.) Not one of these directors subscribed fully to a specific 'method', but most of them were highly efficient and inspiring to work with. They were all faced with a difficult and recurring problem: how to utilise the talents of all the students in the class for the particular production in hand. No one could be left out. Which meant finding a succession of plays where a group of about eighteen students, men and women, could all be profitably engaged. This in turn involved a fair amount of double-casting, with two people rehearsing and playing the same part, with either the one player taking over from the other in the middle of the play, or alternatively each of them doing one or more whole performance. More important, it was mostly impossible to find plays which we really were able to do.

And this brings us to a basic dilemma: artists need to be 'stretched' and challenged, and we only learn by experience. Yet the fact remains that trying to meet a challenge and then failing can be a deeply inhibiting experience (especially in the ambience of the professional training school and in the theatre itself). Also some challenges are best kept out of sight while we build up the experience and skill to cope with them. And the art of choosing a play for any group is to choose material through which they can explore and discover and succeed, not to put them through tests in which they are likely to fail.

How did the different directors at RADA, then, direct? In general they all came to the first rehearsal with their 'moves' for the production fully worked out in advance. Early rehearsals were largely a matter of getting the moves written down, and then going away to learn the lines and the moves together. Casting was done more or less on first impressions; of appearance and personality, and sometimes also of ability in sight-reading the script.

24

As the production evolved, the director would help the actor in a variety of ways. Essentially he would help us firstly to think more fully about what we were doing, and secondly to think more clearly about the particular ways we were doing it and the skills involved. In other words, there would be discussion about:

a   The meaning of what we were saying and doing, within the context of a particular scene, and of the play as a whole. This would be both in the literal sense of what a particular line or action actually means, and also in the more complex sense of what it means within the texture, the rhythm and the mood of a production as a whole.

and also about:

b   The actor's ability actually to do what he thinks he is doing. In the simplest case, if he walks in like a medieval knight in shining armour, or thinks he does, is he actually doing so? In effect the director is here holding up a mirror to the actor, saying 'You're round-shouldered — is this what you mean the character to be?' And so on. And this will include technical matters such as voice and diction.

In helping the actors to achieve the skills necessary for a particular production, the directors at RADA were also teachers — all directors are, anywhere — and they were doing some of the following things, all of them a part of teaching at all times. They were having to

demonstrate   showing what the director means by demonstrating to the actor, performing the action or sequence in the way the director thinks it should be done;

explain   clarifying, discussing and arguing about the meaning of the text;

drill   some of the directors at RADA were especially helpful in giving us particular exercises (usually concerned with diction and vocal projection) which they made us practise again and again at rehearsal;

organise   all directors have to organise the various personnel who go to make up the production team;

inspire   all directors need a charisma, to inspire the company to have faith in them, and to assure the actors in particular that they will not allow them to fail, or to make fools of themselves. In part, such a charisma is also dependent on the company's conviction that the director has done his homework on the text, and that he himself has faith in the company.

In doing all these things, each director works quite differently within the limits of his or her personality. And because each actor is also a personality, so the director who is perfect for one actor may be a disaster for another. Some directors are highly active at rehearsals, getting up all the time to demonstrate and argue. Others are reticent and unobtrusive. Both may achieve excellent results. Some directors are, in fact, retiring almost to a fault, to the point where you can almost fail to notice just how good they are. I remember for instance the tremendous patience of Eve Shapiro, who after carefully 'blocking' *Anne of the Thousand Days*, allowed us a great deal of time and freedom to achieve our own characterisations and interpretations within the framework of her production. She let us move through the rehearsals with a minimum of interruptions and the maximum of encouragement. Her notes at the end of each rehearsal were clear and stimulating, and many of us gained from her a considerable sense of confidence and willingness to experiment with our own ideas.

One director at RADA made a definite point of not only directing, but also of explaining quite extensively *the principles upon which she directed*. This was Mary Duff, with whom I worked on a very good production of André Roussin's comedy *Figure of Fun*. At rehearsal I tried to write down some of her principles as she discussed them with us:

> *on movement on a stage*   use the centre of the stage very sparingly, if at all;
> do not have actors standing in straight lines;
> avoid having two actors move across each other simultaneously;
> do not create symmetrical patterns on the stage;
> *on voice and diction*   the end of a line is more important than the beginning;
> a production must be 'orchestrated', with each actor contributing to a rich variety of tone that fills the ear; then the audience will actually listen and understand;
> *on acting techniques*   act with the other characters, not on your own, and begin by actually looking at them;
> never try to be effective — it's cheap!
> every gesture you make is to be judged by one criterion only: is it absolutely necessary?
> your technique as an actor must always be above the demands of what you are doing at any given moment: then you can act!
> the responsibility of every actor is to make every member of his audience feel better and greater than he ever dreamed he could feel, to feel, 'I belong'.

Miss Duff was really formulating a kind of first exercise in an 'aesthetics of production'. Any such principles are bound to be open to dispute, but probably stimulating and useful even if only because they make us more conscious of the issues involved. All good productions evolve their own aesthetics, their own discipline and economy in the bringing together of actors and text. In each case this will involve certain underlying principles about how the actors move around the stage, how they speak, how the stage 'picture' moves and changes.

I began by suggesting that few institutions actually offer to teach anyone how to direct. But the course at RADA quite effectively did just that, while in fact being designed specifically for the training of actors. Indeed I suspect that the best refresher course for a director is to go and act in somebody else's production.

2 Looking at productions We learn a great deal about our own work by looking sympathetically at the work of others, the good and the bad. For the moment I would like to talk briefly about not only the good, but also the very good.

One of the most remarkable productions I have ever seen was Joan Littlewood's Theatre Workshop production of *Oh What a Lovely War*. This was one of those shows where a great variety of different 'effects' all combine to make a single and forceful impact. The sombre details of the war flashed on to the stage in a series of illuminated news signs, together with music hall numbers and the improvisations of army life, all worked together to shock, amuse and disturb the audience into a new and critical awareness of the 'Great War' and indeed of the whole idea of leadership and power. Isolated moments stand out with particular vividness, such as Avis Bunnage as a music hall performer taking ages and ages to view her audience with forbidding confidence while the band played an introduction which threatened to go on for ever; and the solo tenor voice suddenly ringing out loud and true from amidst the pre-battle church service 'When this lousy war is over, no more soldiering for me!' to the tune of a well-known hymn. It was a moment which all unto itself said more about the ordinary man at war than a thousand books or speeches could hope to do.

In a very different way I have found many of the ballets of Frederick Ashton equally moving, equally powerful, especially the two-act ballets *La Fille mal Gardée* and *The Two Pigeons*. In both these ballets Ashton builds on the skills and expertise of very gifted classical dancers to create something which, like Littlewood's *War*, is unique unto itself; a folk story retold through music and dance, in which a marvellously gentle and restrained sense of pathos and romance is balanced by a strong sense of humour and comedy. The result with both ballets is total theatre,

27

a completely involving drama that endlessly delights and surprises. Sometimes these surprises emanate from the simplest of
devices; for instance contrasting the stage filled with the movement of thirty dancers, with the stage 'filled' with the movement
of only two or even one. Or it may be that one of the dancers
suddenly breaks out of the particular balletic convention that
we think we are watching to do an extremely attractive clog
dance.

So perhaps one of the principal skills which both directors
employ is the ability to move confidently from one convention
to another, and to use them all to create a convention dis-
tinctively their own. Littlewood employs music hall, concert
party, Brechtian alienation (with the device of the newsflashes
as well as with the actors endlessly popping in and out of
character). Ashton employs the convention of classical and
romantic ballet, and then mixes this with pantomime: in *La
Fille* the part of the Mother is played by a man in the best
traditions of the pantomime dame. And Ashton's use of the
corps de ballet to create naturalistic crowd effects, to suggest
ordinary people going about their lives spontaneously and un-
selfconsciously, is closer to the modern musical and straight
theatre than to classical ballet. And indeed Ashton very briefly
breaks right out of the ballet altogether, with the dancers burst-
ing into a kind of improvised song as they dance off the stage.

Ashton is remarkably bold and decisive in creating theatre out
of everything that his particular theatre, the world of ballet, can
offer him. And he is perfectly willing to delight with the most
obvious devices, like the simpleton's umbrella lifting him right
up into the air (flying up and out on a wire) and the heroine's
exit on a cart decked out with flowers and drawn by a pony:
both in *La Fille*. And *The Two Pigeons* ends with two pigeons
flying on to the stage and, with their moves rehearsed, being
incorporated into the very touching and powerful climax of the
drama.

An artist who has something of Ashton's combination of
experimentalism and a sense of convention and tradition (with
each sustaining the other) is the young Japanese musician
Stomu Yamash'ta, whose *Red Buddha Theatre* visited London
briefly in 1973. The nucleus of the Red Buddha troupe is a
small group of actors, musicians and dancers from Japan who
have created under Yamash'ta's direction a theatre which in-
corporates dance and mime, music (especially for the percussion) and the use of masks — a music-theatre in fact, of much
inventiveness and power. In their production *The Man from the
East*, a series of scenes portrayed aspects of the history of Japan
down to modern times. The most moving was a sequence where

two villagers take their old and dying mother up to the top of the mountain to die. The son is sad, but the daughter hardly understands what is happening. Left alone, the mother is enveloped in falling snow, and then, as night falls, the icy spirits of the dead come to carry her off. She struggles for her life, but is finally overcome. The scene was played on a wide open stage, without scenery, but with brilliant soundtrack, creating out of a variety of percussion instruments (drums, cymbals, bells, steel plates, wooden blocks, vibrating rods, etc) and out of the human voice (cries, hums, calls) a marvellously strange and compelling atmosphere. In the climactic moments of the scene, as the mother fought with the spirits, the director used strobe lighting to achieve his effect, with the light flashing on and off in rapid succession, such that each flash of light appeared to the audience to reveal the actors frozen in a new and quite different position on the stage. It made very powerful theatre — marred for me, though, by the amplification of the soundtrack to such a volume that it was at times acutely painful.

Yamash'ta, again, is a perfect instance of the director confidently bridging several traditions; in his case, the tradition of a classically trained musician of great skill, freely exploring rock and jazz to evolve a new form of dance drama.

Equally remarkable in different ways was the work recently seen in London of two directors of straight plays: Ronald Eyre's production of Alan Bennett's play *Habeas Corpus*, and Michael Blakemore's production of Chekov's *The Cherry Orchard*. Blakemore's production sustained a good balance between detail and clarity; all the characters took their time establishing themselves, and changed and evolved as they interacted with one another. The servant Yasha most obviously illustrated this, with the very way he held his shoulders, changing slightly as he dealt with the various people around him, some beneath him in his own view of the social hierarchy, some at his own level and Madame Ranevsky above him. And Constance Cummings captured similar detail in her own performance as Madame: the rather vacuous charm which she dispensed to her entourage, the tendency to stop attending to what was being said, the daydreaming, the sudden transition from laughter to tears and back again to laughter, and then the unexpected moments of toughness and resilience. Small wonder that such a woman, though so foolish in many ways, had somehow survived so incredibly well. And the rich and successful Lopakhin was portrayed by Denis Quilley with an equally clear and convincing range of behaviour: warm and compassionate, yet forceful and proud, sentimental like everyone else yet forward-looking and indeed realistic. All this detail of characterisation was complemented by the lightness of the production in the opening sequences of the play; the well-lit stage, the lightness of movement, the busy-ness of the characters, the bustle and scurrying: if the world were collapsing beneath their feet, they were still getting on quite cheerfully with their existences, and not by any means living in a world of pre-destined gloom. Life was difficult, perhaps, but not awful.

In one detail the production faltered. In the final scene of the play, where the aged servant Firs is unwittingly left behind and locked away, the stage unexpectedly revolved to show Firs in his little bedroom. This was fine, except that throughout his final speech Firs was invisible to the audience on either extreme side of the theatre, for the walls of the bedroom effectively concealed his face from view. In this way the final impact of the play was completely muffled.

Where Blakemore's production was leisurely and detailed, Eyre's production of *Habeas Corpus* was bold and simple and unambiguous. From the very opening of the play, with the sound of a cinema organ blaring forth (such that some of us in the audience did actually lean forward expecting to see the organist ascend smilingly through the floor in front of the stage) the director sustained the 'we're having a treat' quality that is an essential part of the play. The excellent company of actors knew without exception the precise degree of caricature to which they could go without upsetting the balance of the play, and the quickness of pace and deftness of movement were maintained throughout. The writing is skilful and also difficult; the central character must create a naturalism, an ordinary reality, while everyone else is a farcical 'type', such that finally the fate of the central character is the fate of 'everyman', and a sad and disturbing fate at that. But writer, director and actor (Alec Guinness) achieved this balance fully and very powerfully. Indeed one of the skills which both Blakemore and Eyre brought to their productions was the capacity to create a framework within which their very experienced and skilful actors were able to evolve their performances. The virtuosity of such artists is a part of the very essence of the production, and not just an extra added to the top of it. And again, in this as in the other ways about which I have talked earlier, the director is a teacher, creating the right framework to liberate the talent of the actors.

3 Directing The director in 'the theatre' versus the director in 'education'. In talking about my own experience as a director, I am brought up against the whole business of the teacher/ lecturer/director in schools, colleges, universities and acting academies, for my own work as a director has been exclusively in schools and colleges of one kind or another. There are very substantial differences between directing companies inside the theatrical profession and outside it, and since the majority of directors at any one time are almost certainly *outside* the professional theatre, it will be useful to dwell for a moment on some of these differences. When talking of the non-professional director, I have in mind especially:

a   The teacher working in schools and producing school plays of one kind or another.

b   The teacher/lecturer in drama schools directing both students who wish to become professional actors, and students who (in increasing numbers) go to such schools to train as teachers of drama.

c   The teacher/lecturer directing students as part of the work on drama courses at colleges and universities, and sometimes students who are not involved in studying drama but who wish to work with the director on some kind of extra-curricular basis. I include here the work done in colleges for the training of teachers (and not just of drama teachers).

d   The director of the work done by independent amateur groups of all kinds. A great deal of what I say about the director in education applies equally to the director in such companies which are outside entirely any educational institution.

The main differences between the director working with professionals and the director working in educational/amateur groups seem to be that in the latter case:

a   The director is specifically employed as a *teacher*.

b   The company working under him are students, and not necessarily students of drama. Even where they are students who hope to enter the acting profession, they are still beginners and in a learning situation.

c   Very often *all* the members of the company, and not just the actors, are students also. Therefore the director must be able to teach them too — designers, lighting men, stage managers, and so on.

d   Whereas most professional companies are specifically assembled for a production or productions, with each member chosen for his particular talent, companies in educational contexts are usually assembled for other purposes. Generally, a student gets on to a college/university course through skills other than as an actor, usually through academic skills. Of course, even within a college, a specific company may be chosen with a particular production in mind, but it seems to me that here the teacher acting as director (as opposed to the student acting as director) must proceed with great care. If he follows the precedent of the professional theatre and creates theatre out of elite groups — where people are auditioned, say, or chosen by some weeding-out process — then this can work very strongly against what most of us mean by *educational*. The task of the director in schools, colleges and the like is not to find a small band of potentially fine talent and concentrate on that, but to keep the doors wide open to the greatest possible numbers of people who may be intrigued to come along. Only in this way will students and pupils who are not 'theatrical' ever come to an experience of making theatre. This means very great care and skill in choosing the play.

The amateur group outside of education can have an advantage over both the professional and the educational group: it is often possible for amateur groups to institutionalise themselves and to work together over a very long period of time. This is only rarely possible in the profession, and in education not at all, for the student population is always changing. Even so, of course, a group of students may stay together for a period of say two or three productions. The extent to which people know each other through working together is bound to make an immense impact upon the kind of productions that can be embarked upon. In educational groups, the director-teacher will find that he is repeatedly having to start teaching again from the beginning, creating theatre out of very inexperienced talent to whom a large amount of elementary teaching must be given. This is the basic factor of his work. This does not mean that he will be unable to create very varied theatre out of the talent around him, or that he cannot be an extremely versatile teacher.

The work I have done as a director-teacher in schools and colleges has been influenced by all the five factors I have just outlined. At no time have I taught drama students, but rather students of a great variety of subjects who briefly became caught up in the idea of creating a production with me, working in a large and varied team. While I have worked often in a more or less specialist capacity as a drama teacher, my students and pupils have been mostly non-specialist. And the best work I have done in creating theatre has been extra-curricular for all concerned, including myself, ie every one has worked voluntarily in their own spare time. By and large my experience has been that a large number of students/pupils want to partake of a production if given half a chance, and that they are capable of learning an enormous amount from such work even though they may have very modest abilities or potential as performers. In general, I have not had the companies with whom I felt I could do great plays, though once or twice it would have been possible for me to take out a small group of performers from the school or college group, to direct them in such a play. So far, I have resisted the temptation, and have rather taken the line that where there is a small sub-group of remarkable talent, then this is a golden opportunity for a student to direct the group himself. My task is to work with as many as possible, in as open a situation as possible, to give the maximum number an experience of making theatre if they are prepared to give up the time that is involved. This does not necessarily imply a sharp division between small-cast plays and extravaganzas, epics and the like. The kind of work which I see as part of the drama teacher's role, I also see as non-elitist, non-exclusive. As a consequence, a great deal of the work I have directed has been in the terrain of the extravaganza and the improvised production. (I discuss one of them in a later chapter.) This has enabled me to extend opportunities to a great range of talents and people; not only acting talent, but dancing, gymnastic, singing, writing, and so on.

Sometimes the problem of 'choosing the play' is seen within the context of an argument: education versus professional training. For instance, it is still often said that the teacher in the drama school must choose material where he can train his actors, while the teacher in the non-professional school or college has the luxury of being able to think simply of educating his actors, meaning by this, he can concentrate on a great variety of possible texts and material without having to worry whether or not the actor is really learning *to act.*

The answers to such an argument would include, for me, two particular points: first, that all experience of making theatre, if it is lively and committed theatre, total theatre, is bound to be good for any actor, whether amateur or professional. Good theatre is good education for all those who are involved in it, including the audience. Conversely, poor theatre is un-educational, even when housed in an educational institution. Secondly, poor theatre often emanates from a desire to do too much too soon, to do great plays when the actors simply do not have the experience to do them. And frequently this follows from the erroneous view that it is only by doing such plays that actors can ever learn to act. Or alternatively, that simply nothing else is worth doing.

Theories of theatre

The theatre has always been bedevilled by the urge to imitate what the top professional theatre is doing. Thus the majority of touring professional companies and resident repertory companies have always largely confined themselves to a staple diet of West End successes, and most amateur companies up and down the land have followed in their footsteps. Meanwhile, the West End to a very large extent goes on imitating its own self.

It is against this kind of decadence that new writers, new directors, new companies and new theatres have attempted to protest. And out of such work, new theories of theatre have evolved. The theatre of — the absurd; cruelty; action; the living newspaper; commitment; social realism; psychotherapy; socio-therapy; ontological hysteria.[5] Any such list is bound to leave out some of the best experimental work being done, and indeed the very names of such theatres are equally bound to mislead, partly because they tend to imply an unreal degree of exclusive-ness, and partly because what they are trying to achieve cannot be summed up in a single word — 'cruelty' for instance. What is important is that there is a great deal of experimental work going on. Equally important, all of it is worth supporting and looking at. No doubt many experiments will come to nothing; perhaps what looks staggeringly new right now, will be judged eventu-ally as extremely conventional. When Pinero wrote *The Second Mrs Tanqueray* it must have seemed an extraordinarily new kind of play, pointing the way to a new and exciting kind of theatre. But it appears just a very ordinary, very accomplished, well-made play by most modern standards. No doubt too, with the passage of time, many of today's experiments will be entirely forgotten and only a small number will endure. But that does not invalidate the work that does *not* endure. Nor does it mean that whatever makes exciting theatre now will also make ex-citing theatre tomorrow or next year. The criterion is, what does it do to us, here and now?

All experiments provide an important service without which the theatre as an art form would disappear. They create oppor-tunities for new talent. They open the doors for creativity. This is true not only of the practical work of the people who in one way or another actually make theatre, but also of the work, of the theorist (who also is usually caught up in trying to make theatre as a practitioner). The theorist seeks to publicise the idea behind the experiment, and sometimes, of course, may be writing in advance of any practical work. His task is bound to be a difficult one, partly because a theory must translate some-thing into words, which, in the case of the theatre, will be only *partly* verbal. The theatrical production is an amalgam of sounds and movements, of which the word itself may well be a very modest part. As a result the theory may seem unduly portentous and difficult, if not downright pretentious, for the theory can only be meaningful at the point where you translate it into the images of the theatre itself. Indeed there is a basic difficulty in using the very word 'theory' in the context of any art form, and most especially of theatre, for objective modes of proof, on which a theory is normally thought to rest, are simply not present.[6]

Perhaps the most influential of modern theorists of the theatre is the French writer Antonin Artaud, usually considered the father of the theatre of cruelty. Artaud was deeply concerned that the theatre should escape from what he saw as the monotony and degradation of the conventional theatre, and should achieve its full service to the public as a 'restorer of life'. He argues that man's humanity, man's compassion, emanate from an awareness of the pain and cruelty that his lack of humanity and compassion can cause him to inflict upon others. And the role of the theatre is to show the audience such cruelty that they will go away purged of the desire to inflict cruelty upon others. Through being shocked into an awareness of the pain of life, they will seek to reduce rather than add to the pain. Artaud expresses it in this way:

'Whatever conflicts may obsess the mentality of the times, I defy any spectator infused with the blood of violent scenes, who has felt higher actions pass through him, who has seen the rare, fundamental motions of his thought illuminated in extraordinary events — violence and bloodshed having been placed at the service of violence in thought — once outside the theatre, I defy him to indulge in thoughts of war, riot or motiveless murder.'[7]

Artaud is never easy to follow, but it seems that he is here stating in a more extreme form the view which many of us would accept, and which is fully explored in the writings of, for instance, Suzanne Langer, that the experiences we have second-hand, through plays, films, novels, all have a profound influence on our thinking and therefore on our morality. The pain we experience in this way, also second-hand, teaches us to avoid inflicting and causing such pain in real life.

What kind of theatre does Artaud seek to create, in order to achieve this purging of cruelty through cruelty in the theatre? He asks for:

'a theatre where violent physical images pulverise, mesmerise the audience's sensibilities, caught up in the drama as if in a vortex of higher forces.'[8]

And how does he define the word 'cruelty'?:

'I use the word cruelty in the sense of hungering after life, cosmic strictness . . . the inescapable necessary pain without which life could not continue.'[9]

And how will this theatre be achieved? He advocates merging

the role of author and director into one, and the employment not only of language but of all possible forms of scenery, movement, action, music, costume and lighting.[10] In particular he advocates the rewriting and refashioning of existing plays, and in so doing incidentally aligns himself with other theorists such as Brecht and Grotowski,[11] while also incurring the wrath of those who deplore any rethinking of the classics. I suspect though that Artaud is absolutely right, and that some of the most exciting theatre grows out of experimental rethinking of existing texts.

The vitality of Artaud's thinking is evidenced in the extent of his influence — and my brief summary of his ideas is meant only to serve as an introduction. No doubt the work he has already inspired will itself inspire many others, and will spark off new departures and new protests against itself. I would only suggest at this point that Artaud's thinking appears to rule out altogether the kind of theatre which is of escape rather than confrontation, of delight and humour rather than pain. And people very clearly need a theatre which offers them this release, this escape, this interlude if you like, from the serious business of living. There is an important place, very obviously, for *My Fair Lady*, for *Private Lives*, for *Godspell*, and I for one cannot imagine life, or the theatre, without them.

The stages of a production

Productions will usually progress through various stages:
1   The initial idea, tentatively working it out, and then co-ordinating with other personnel, especially those concerned with lighting, scenic design, costume and stage management.
2   Early rehearsals: prior to working on the text there may well be a period in which the director and the company talk about the play and about its acting and production. This may involve looking at the social and historical context, at written documents, at films, paintings, etc. In discussing his production of the Maxim Gorky plays for The Royal Shakespeare Company, David Jones suggests that the company should do any reading together, with each reading a paragraph to the rest, and then talking about it with the others.[12]

After this preliminary work, the company will then either read the play together sitting down (not always a valuable exercise) or at once start moving (or 'blocking') the play. This will usually be quite a slow process, to enable the actors to get all their moves clearly written down as the director gives them. (Certainly there will be a great deal of time wasted if actors do not write the moves down, for needless to say they are otherwise extremely difficult to remember.)

Blocking is not absolutely essential, and some directors work without specifying to the actors or fixing their particular moves at any one time. In such instances the movements are evolved through experiment at rehearsal and at performances also. At one extreme is the director who refuses ever to block any play, regarding it as a calculated infanticide of the company's talents and of the production. At the other is the director who works out every move before the first rehearsal and then refuses ever to alter it.

Bernard Shaw suggested that the director work out his moves using a chess board to represent the stage and the pieces to represent the actors. In this way you can see clearly where any actor is at any one time. Certainly there are many plays where it is impossible to imagine a production working without being very carefully blocked; farces in particular, and especially a farce such as Joe Orton's *Loot* where there is such a vast amount of business with props and furniture.

3   Coming to grips with the text: at all rehearsals there will be numerous problems revolving around the meaning and interpretation of the text, and the translating of the text into action, into theatre. Noël Coward reportedly summed up the whole business of rehearsing with the cryptic advice to 'learn your lines and don't bump into the furniture!' This, in other words, less elegant, is the expression of the 'outside-in' school of acting and directing: get the external framework right, and then work out the internals on your own. The work of Stanislavsky, and of the Method Studio in New York, represent the opposite, the 'inside-out' school: the actor must progress from his own understanding of the text (which will involve a great deal of preliminary talk and improvisation) towards the text itself (with further talk and improvisation) and then, finally, towards the actual business of production. Either school can be taken to the extreme. Most companies effect a useful compromise between the two, in which a framework is created *while* there is still a lot of talk and argument going on.

A good example comes again from David Jones, talking about his work with the Royal Shakespeare Company:

> 'The key thing I'm interested in with actors is them expanding their intellectual and emotional horizon — basically, getting them to trust their vulnerability, which is to do with playing together as well as on their own, which is to do with the part being fresh each night . . .'[13]

And the director he says, will often be saying to the actors:

> 'That could be taken further, you're near that, but actually I

don't quite believe you're interested in that situation.'

In exploring the text with the actors, Jones explains that he does not ask the actors to improvise situations in their own words. He gives two reasons for this. First,

'I'm much more interested in trying to release the actors on the text, by actually sticking with those words, because I believe that the words themselves often open doors.'

And secondly, with the specific plays that he is discussing, Maxim Gorky's,

'There is a kind of Edwardian style about their way of talking, where if it is translated into modern terms you're actually losing nuances.'

4   The middle period of rehearsals will involve continued chances to argue and experiment, as well as to consolidate. There will need to be runthroughs where there are no inter-ruptions, as well as others where the work is stopped to allow discussion and exploration of specific problems as they occur.
5   Final rehearsals will include technical runthroughs and re-hearseals for lighting, sound effects, etc, as well, of course, as full dress rehearsals (as many as possible) at which all the aspects of the production are brought together. It is up to the director and his company to decide whether they want an audience at the dress rehearsals, but there should generally be no question of admitting any kind of audience at earlier re-hearsals. A rehearsal is an exercise, a lesson, an experiment, in which an audience can either embarrass or distract the actor from the business in hand and push him prematurely towards giving a performance.

It may be worth adding, by way of post script, that directing is essentially one side of the coin, of which acting is the other side. And so whatever is said about the one is complemented by what is said about the other.

3 The Actor

Of all aspects of dramatic craft, acting looks the easiest. Designing the scenery; building the scenery; lighting the production; making the costumes: almost everyone would acknowledge the part played by sheer skill and effort in all such enterprises. But when it comes to the actor presenting himself on the stage, the vast majority of the public seem to be not only unimpressed by the achievement of the actor but also highly suspicious of his motives. I remember the comment of one member of staff in a large comprehensive school where I taught some years ago. The drama group were presenting an extremely ambitious musical extravaganza involving a cast of forty pupils and a backstage company of twenty or so more. But this particular teacher was not moved at all by the mere social demands that an enterprise of this size makes upon all its members, and even less so by the artistic demands. 'It's just an excuse for kids to show off', he explained good naturedly. 'You put those kids back in the classroom and you'll see their true colours.' And he added, in case the point was not yet absolutely clear, 'Most of them are delinquents. That's why acting appeals to them.'

In less exaggerated form, this seems to be the attitude of a goodly number of people, to whom acting is a form of exhibitionism, where the only quality that divides those who can and do from those who cannot and will not is the sheer effrontery involved in getting on to the stage in the first place. No doubt this is in part just another symptom of the inherent distrust with which all the arts are held in our culture. And maybe this helps to explain why even now, when drama is tentatively establishing itself in the ordinary curriculum of the schools, drama teachers are so often at pains to reject all association with theatre and performance and production, and instead hitch their wagon with absolute insistence to theories of 'child development' and 'mental health'. It perhaps explains too, why amateur theatre is so often held up to ridicule: professional theatre is bad enough, but amateur is a total affront to the puritan ethic, implying as it does, that people will get together to create drama without any hope of glory or of financial reward.

In part too, the generally low rating of the actor's craft is related to the very different kinds of activity that can legitimately be called acting. He who plays the king has to take his place alongside the swimming champion who is enlisted by Hollywood to play Tarzan, and alongside the curly-haired 'poppet' of five years old who, the press solemnly inform us, acts all the mature professionals off the screen and out into the alley at the back of the Roxy. They are all acting. But in terms of the kinds of skill involved, they are not really doing the same thing at all.

Nor do I mean to imply that all these various activities are not worth while. The actor who spends an entire career, and perhaps a highly lucrative one too, turning in the same performance in play after play, film after film, is fulfilling an important function for his public, as is the glamorous young lady whose beauty suddenly makes a spectacular impact on the cinema screen. Indeed one of the numerous fascinations of looking at actors is that it reveals so many very different kinds of talent, all of them important. By and large, for instance, the different media demand different kinds of acting, and different kinds of actor. Remarkably few film actors have been able to make the transition from screen to stage with particular success, and even the traffic in the opposite direction has not been especially intense or remarkable. Similarly, television has tended quite rightly to create its own actors with their own techniques, their own particular talents, their own appeal. Of course, there are those who have mastered with ease all the different media (radio included), and perhaps these are the true virtuosi of the acting profession. But they are the exceptions.

Similarly, even within the limits of the conventional theatre, and within the limits of, say, one particular company, very few actors can be expected to be able to do almost anything. Most actors are, by the very nature of things, going to achieve excellence within a more or less narrow field: they are never going to play Romeo to their own satisfaction or to their audience's, nor even Mercutio! Yet drama academies continue to operate on the assumption that there is so much that *all* actors must be able to do, and indeed I have not yet come across one such institution which dares to offer its students any significant degree of choice as to the subjects they are expected to study. The sole exception is the classes in singing, which are usually offered as an optional extra, rather than as an alternative to anything else. But a subject like fencing is invariably a compulsory subject for all students, regardless of the fact that very many actors of very considerable talent will never, in a thousand years, be able to engage in a sword fight, on stage or off, with any degree of confidence or skill.

Is it possible, then, to think of such a widely varied activity as acting in terms of basic skills which are actually basic to all acting? If we narrow the field to stage acting then it seems we can reasonably suggest that the skills which the actor must develop fall into five categories. All these categories overlap, and it could be said that the last three are no more than the ways in which the first two are employed. But all of them will need to be studied, in one way or another, by all actors.

The basic skills

1 Movement An acting performance presents a series of moving images to the audience, and it is largely by the quality of his movement that the audience interprets the kind of person that the actor is portraying, and the significance of what he says and does. On stage, as in life, the movement tells all, or very nearly so. Thus the romantic lover who fumbles his way to his mistress's bedside belies the passion inherent in both his words and his actions, as does the sword-fighter who somehow contrives to miss the bravado in the lines the author has given him; some feature of his movement, however intangible, fails to signify the total confidence and aggressiveness that the words demand.

The intelligent actor knows when his movement is inadequate to the task in hand, and the over-sensitive actor can need endless reassurance from everyone even when he is in fact doing perfectly well. But in any event, the actor knows that if he is to play the part at all, he must feel it is right in his body, in his muscles, in his every move.

This is often misrepresented as an intellectual factor, rather than a kinaesthetic one: by which I mean that actors are often accused of failing to understand or of misinterpreting an author's intentions, when in fact their failing has nothing to do with a correct reading of the text, or indeed anything to do with intellect or intelligence as such. The actor has read the play with great sympathy and insight, but simply cannot translate the character into movement. He could quite possibly, though, write an absolutely accurate essay on the same character. The most obvious instances of this occur when playing characters, such as Othello and Cleopatra, who recognisably have distinctive movement, but the problem is in fact present all the time. Every character moves in a unique fashion. If you analyse the people you know, looking not only at the broad features of their movement, the way they walk, the way they eat, the way they do their work, but also at the more incidental and unconscious aspects of their movement (often referred to as *shadow moves*) then you are left in each case with a complex pattern peculiar to each individual. And the actor must seek to capture all of these characteristics, down to the use of the hands, the movement of the muscles of the face, the way of smiling, the way of looking, the way of responding. Indeed it is often in the playing of the small parts, and the crowd parts, that the failure to *move* in character is most apparent and therefore most distracting.

Part of the complexity of our movement, and the study of it, is that the conscious and the unconscious overlap, and because of this the image we create, the personality we present to others, is itself a partly unconscious mechanism. We never quite know how we strike others, what we appear to be, and even when we are most in control of ourselves we also reveal aspects of ourselves without either intending to, or being aware that we are doing so. And it is our movement (even more than what we say) which gives the game away. This alone makes it difficult for the actor, for he must be able to convey both aspects of the character's movement: the intended and also the unintended. But it is more difficult even than this, for he must also control his own movement, must somehow ensure that the unconscious features of his movement come under his control, and do not work against the character that he is portraying.

It is perhaps because of this, that the commercial theatre goes in for 'type casting', which really means that the actor is chosen because to a greater extent than even he perhaps realises, all the incidental aspects of his movement suggest the character he is to play.

2   Voice and speech   Similarly the actor must capture the appropriate quality of voice and speech, of tone and pitch, of accent, rhythm and diction. And in many classical roles he will need considerable skill in the control of breathing so as to handle the demands of long and sustained speeches without running out of breath.

3   Imagination   The skills of movement and voice and speech are as nothing to the actor unless he has also the imagination with which to use them. An unimaginative actor is a contradiction in terms, yet the word itself, 'imagination', remains a singularly difficult one to define with any kind of accuracy. One thing seems reasonably clear: when we respond well to an actor's performance, then his imagination sparks off our own. We are stimulated. We ourselves become, and enjoy feeling, imaginative. The images created by the actor on the stage not only evoke recognition, but call forth a hundred other associations and images from us, the audience. Such is the excitement of looking at drama, of going to the theatre. One might say that the creativity of the artist makes the audience creative as well.

Many of the arguments one hears about whether or not the actor is a *creative* artist seem to miss the point about the job the actor is performing. Working with the written script provided by the author, and within the framework laid down by the production, he must create life on the stage. The sounds, the movement, the appearance, the meaning of the words: all these are created afresh by each actor each time he plays the part. No two performances even by the same person can ever be quite identical.

In evolving his performance, the actor does what all artists and all thinkers have to do: he experiments. He tries out this and that. He dares to go too far. He even makes a fool of himself. He experiences the same problem as the writer experienced when he was writing the play: am I stretching the audience's sensibilities too far — Or not far enough? Am I exceeding their imaginative limits? or am I not even within striking distance of so doing? Sometimes this problem is represented as one of finding the reality, the inner truth. But even this is rendered complicated by the fact that major artists of all kinds are those who break through the accepted bounds of what is considered true and real, and in this way actually extend our knowledge, our understanding. And this is true as much of actors as of other artists; the great ones have almost literally shocked us into a new awareness, such that in certain ways we never think and feel in quite the same way again.

I have already suggested that 'imagination' is a term that defies definition. Psychologists have battled for the last fifty years or so to pin it down, but the word remains elusive. We recognise the phenomenon itself, we know, for instance, when a performance or a play is imaginative, but as soon as we start defining what the imagination is, we get caught up with roughly similar yet not identical terms such as 'thinking', 'instinct', 'feeling' and 'behaviour'.

But if we do not know *what* it is, we do know a great deal *about* it. And much of what we know comes from those who, by general agreement, have or had considerable imagination. Some of the things we know about highly imaginative people may seem pedestrian, but for anyone endeavouring to master an art such as acting (or indeed any other imaginative activity) it will be useful to spell them out.

First of all, it is clear from almost everything we know about highly creative people that they are also highly industrious and conscientious. In plain language, they are not afraid of hard work. Noël Coward, for example, may well have cultivated a veneer of coolness, of effortless spontaneity, but it is obvious from the sheer volume of his output that his talent to amuse was only matched by his capacity for work. The fact that he managed to write a masterpiece of theatre in three days should not blind us to the fact he also devoted day after day, year after year, to creative endeavour which did not all add up to 'master-pieces' but which did mean that at the time of his most important output he was a fully practised and experienced craftsman. In other words, what was achieved in three days was in fact achieved over a very long period of time.

Bernard Shaw makes this very clear in his admirable *Advice to a Young Critic*, where he repeatedly points out that is is only by writing and writing, every day, as a mere exercise, that Shaw the dramatist has acquired his expertise.[14]

Secondly, it seems that all kinds of experience may stimulate the artist in his work, the wider the range the better. And indeed to a considerable extent, the experiences that will so stimulate him are unpredictable, and may affect him without his knowing it. There are many interesting examples of this in Peter McKellar's *Imagination and Thinking* where the work of a number of poets is studied with a view to tracing the possible sources of some of their imagery. What influenced them, perhaps unconsciously, to write this poem — to choose this image — to write that particular line in that particular way? Of course, no conclusive answer can be made, but definite influences can be ascertained. For example, a visit to a country house while Keats was about to write *The Eve of St Agnes* seems to have influenced very con-siderably the imagery the poet employed. Similarly, poets who never travelled across the English Channel have been affected by even the most superficial writings about distant places, and have created remarkable portraits of lands they have never seen. What we read, what we see, what we hear, what we do: every-thing may contribute to the experience from which we create our own work. As Peter McKellar points out, everything is created out of something. Nothing comes from nowhere. Nor is the possible list of source material limited to those experiences which we encounter consciously: dreams, daydreams and fantasies are also significant.[15]

It is this very fact which explains the age-old equation of the artist with non-conformity, with Bohemianism, with anarchism and protest; every society, every epoch finds a new name for it. Because the artist cannot settle for what he already knows, he must endlessly seek new experience, new wisdom. As soon as he settles, he is done for. He is no longer learning. When the horizon no longer expands, then it starts to diminish. Writers such as Shaw and Ibsen have dramatised the dilemma with great force and eloquence, Shaw with optimism, and Ibsen with (in general) Nordic pessimism. Shaw's heroes tend to fight the whole idea of settling down, of conforming, and also to win at least a few major battles in the process; while Ibsen's heroes are as likely as not to lose everything. But, of course, both sides of the coin represent the truth.

Phrased slightly differently, the artist's pursuit of new knowledge, new experience, becomes the cult and worship of excess. Everything must be taken too far, and indeed too far can never be far enough. One can never live too much. The point is illustrated not only in the work of many artists, Shaw and Wilde, for instance, but also in their lives. The amount of time that Shaw himself spends writing, and advocates others to spend if they wish to achieve his level of skill and proficiency, is itself excessive, and absurd even, unless one justifies it by the value one attaches to what he writes.

So the creative artist is one who works hard and lives fully, even excessively. He is also one who presents his work to the public. When an artist succeeds, there is a shared feeling between the artist and his audience which can be deeply exciting and disturbing to both. Generally, this shared feeling is seen as a hit or miss and even anarchic activity, without rhyme or reason. But in her fascinating study of the impact of a work of art upon its public, Suzanne Langer in *Philosophical Sketches* suggests that works of art are as much the product of rational thought as are works of science and philosophy. Their distinction and uniqueness is that they find their rationality not in the laws of objective thinking but in the laws of *subjective* thinking, and that these are in fact the laws of the imagination. The actor on the stage is portraying and revealing subjective truths, perceived and expressed through the imagination. Where science speaks of the world outside us, art speaks of the world inside, of the experience of living, or better still, of the world of feeling. The arts speak to us of what it feels like to be alive. As soon as the element of *feeling* is diminished or abolished, then art is no longer involved. A spectacle will quite rightly elicit sensations in the observer, but only a work of art will elicit feelings. Suzanne Langer notes that a circus, for instance, may grip and shock its audience, but there is no expression of felt experience. And thus, a work of art in performance may cease to be art, if the performer impresses with his virtuosity, but fails to express the feeling that the original writer has sought to embody in the work. This can easily happen where, for instance, extracts are performed. I am thinking here not only of dramatic recitals, but also of the kind of programmes which Russian ballet companies are especially fond of performing while they are on tour: these tend to consist of highlights from great ballets and to involve what one might call instant impact, with the dancers no sooner on the stage than they are performing feats of fantastic skill and difficulty. The result is more like a high-class gymkhana than a work of art.[16]

But the same phenomenon can be seen even within the framework of the production of a complete work. The actor may give a superficially fine performance, with everything right and proper, yet we are not moved, not touched, not concerned. The spectacle is right, but in the final analysis, nothing is shared between the actor and his audience. Nor is this necessarily the same thing as over-acting. The actor who overdoes it, who goes over the top, will inevitably lose the truth of what he is doing, but the actor who is not guilty on this score may even so contribute to the same thing: the loss of feeling between the actor and his audience.

It was this very fact which Stanislavsky thought about most carefully. And indeed the central concern of his work is that the actor should find the technique with which he can not only capture the feeling of being the character in the play, but also be able to recapture and express that feeling at every performance, so that there is never a time when the audience is denied the real experience of that particular work of art. The actor always feels the experience, and so does the audience. I look briefly at Stanislavsky's theory of acting a little later in this chapter.

4 Projection   The fact that the actor's work is essentially a sharing activity, involving the audience as well, underlines the role of projection in the making up of the actor's skill and technique. Not only must he be heard, he must also be perceived, and understood. He may quite possibly be feeling all the right things, but if this does not reach the audience it is of no value at all. The importance of projection has a phenomenal effect upon the actor's entire technique, and does much to explain the difference between acting on the stage and on the cinema screen. In particular, it dictates for the stage actor a tremendous sense of discipline and of simplicity; the more you try to do at any one time, the more likely you are to convey and to project either nothing or else a confusion. And so a sense of economy of movement and gesture becomes second nature to most actors, and is essential in order to underline for the audience (and so to project) those gestures and movements which are significant. Indeed, this sense of economy is fundamental to all art forms. For the actor on the stage it is dictated by three basic questions: if what I am now doing matters to the audience, then can I be seen — can I be heard — can I be understood?

It should be added that being heard and being understood are not necessarily the same thing. This point can be most cruelly illustrated by the small-part player in Shakespeare, when he charges on to announce some highly dramatic offstage event, often at considerable length, leaving us, after he has made his exit, none the wiser as to the purpose of his visit.

5 Team-work And finally, all the actor's skills are of no use if he is unable to bring to them a further skill, of being able to work with other people. It is a skill which nowadays is more discussed and studied than ever before, by everyone from social psychologists and management consultants to union leaders and politicians. By and large, in my personal experience, actors work together very well. In the non-professional theatre, those who do not like the team quickly withdraw from it; and in the profession itself, a basic part of the pleasure of the work, when you can get it, is the experience of doing something worthwhile with other actors; the chance, in other words, to join a good team. There are exceptions, of course, and probably every acting company has its more or less full-time moaner, groaner and scandal-monger, usually operating at a safe distance from the people at whom the moans and groans are being directed. I have also known at least one instance of an actor of very considerable skill, who made a disaster of his professional career because he was unable to work successfully with other people. He had all the requisite skills except the social one.

In essence, good team-work rests on mutual sympathy and concern. In other words, it has much to do with an awareness of the problems of other people, and not only of one's own problems; an awareness that the director, the stage management, the lighting crew, the other actors (and even the author himself) are faced with difficulties, and that they deserve one's consideration and assistance. Actors who cannot see this are destructive to the company and to the work of the company.

Theories of acting

Most of us tend to be suspicious of theories unless they happen to relate to combustion engines, the stars at night, or to some other inhuman or super-human phenomenon. When they relate to humans themselves, we become sceptical, and when they relate to actors (or any other kind of artist) we are as likely as not to be downright contemptuous. All of this is rather unfair to the theorist, for all he has done has been to assemble a great

47

range of ideas into a more or less coherent form and invite us to put them into practice, to try them out. When these ideas seem to produce useful results with a fair number of practitioners, then we can sensibly call that group of ideas a theory. This does not mean that every single time any actor uses the theory he will achieve the wished-for result. Indeed, very few of the theories employed in medicine, in physics or in engineering (let alone in economics or in government) ever achieve any kind of in-built guarantee or infallibility, but this does not invalidate their usefulness or importance. Similarly, a theory of acting may prove quite meaningless to one actor, and yet highly fruitful and inspiring to another. And indeed a great deal of the theory may become part of the common sense and common parlance of the theatre, so that an actor employs a theory without in fact realising that he does so.

I would like to look briefly at three quite different theories which have made and are making an impact upon modern actors.

Stanislavsky is the logical first choice, since his impact has been as yet the most extensive and the most widely publicised.

Part of the difficulty in understanding Stanislavsky's work lies in the enormous range of his thinking and his writing. The other difficulty, for me at least, lies in the apparent lack of humour with which he relates his experiences in the theatre; much of his writing is autobiographical and deals with his work in the training and directing of actors, as well as with the analysis of his own work as both actor and director. Yet it tends to make solemn reading. Perhaps the culture barrier proves as divisive as the Iron Curtain.

Because he ranges so far and wide, and looks back at such a rich store of living and working, his thinking constantly changes and constantly shifts its ground. No sooner have you spotted the central feature of his thinking than you discover you are mistaken. On the printed page he is not unlike the real-life director on the stage: what he said yesterday has been discarded to make way for a new insight, a new philosophy. The result can be exhausting as well as invigorating. But there is no denying the ambitiousness of his writings, and the passionate endeavour to get down on to paper the great complexity of his experience in staging and producing the play. His books remain a marvellous treasure-trove of ideas, experience and advice.

The basis of his thinking seems to be along these lines:
1   The actor must fully understand the text on which he is working.
2   He must fully understand himself also, and be able to forge all kinds of imaginative links between himself and the text.

3   The techniques which Stanislavsky suggests for reaching such an understanding of both the text and of oneself, will also enable the actor to recharge his batteries, so to speak, almost at will. Thus the attributes which enable one to act, including the unconscious attributes, come fully under the actor's control. Then he need never to give an uninspired performance.

How is such understanding achieved?

First, Stanislavsky suggests, the actor must see the text in terms of action. Acting is doing: a character is always doing something to somebody, and the business of comprehending a script is largely a matter of clarifying to oneself what is actually being done at any given moment, by whom, to whom and against what resistance. But the character on the stage, like the individual in real life, will be doing or acting on various levels at the same time. There will be a surface action, such as making a cup of tea, with various undertones and intentions lying at the heart of it, such as seeking to seduce the girl-friend or poison the lodger in order to get hold of his money. All such inner layers of the action, which Stanislavsky calls the sub-text, will be expressed not only in the broad scope of the actions performed by the character, but also in the various details of gesture and movement that accompany it: in the incidental and perhaps unconscious movement of the eyes, the hands, the face, the whole body.

To understand these actions, the actor must also explore the motivation for them. *What* the character does is bound up with *why* he does it. The motivation too will have various levels: in part it will be unconscious.

But neither action nor motivation can really be understood by the actor except in relation to himself. Very often, the relationship will be obvious and apparent to the actor. At other times, the parallels between the actor's experience of life and the experiences of the character in the play may be difficult to find. In the latter instance, it will help the actors for all of them to discuss together even the remotest parallels in their own lives, and if possible to improvise them as a company, to act out a spontaneous drama around them. This will help to establish imaginative links between the text and the players.

Improvisation will also help to deepen the understanding of the text itself and to clarify to the actors the actions they are performing. And so Stanislavsky advocates that the company, having discussed what is happening in a particular scene, should then attempt to improvise the actions in their own words. Out of all this a greater perception will come, and a greater imaginative involvement.

All of this work is, for Stanislavsky, highly detailed, not just generalised. The actor must worry his way, and work his way, and argue and discuss and improvise his way, until he comes through to a performance that feels right (to the director as well as to himself) for that particular production. By this time, he will have created within himself a complex series of responses to the text and to the production which will sustain him through any number of performances. He will have created in his own imagination a character of such richness and complexity that he will, in fact, have more inspiration than he will ever actually need. There will always be something in reserve. He will know, for instance, all about the character's previous life. He will know what the character was doing before he walked on to the stage. He will *feel like* the character. And this great store of feeling will sustain him and inspire him. At the point where it fails to do so, he will go back to the beginning, and argue and discuss and improvise all over again.

Numerous criticisms can be levelled at Stanislavsky's theory. Perhaps the most incisive has come from Theodore Komisarjevsky, who knew and worked with him. Komisarjevsky's major complaint is that the whole idea of drawing on one's own personal experience (of relating to what Stanislavsky calls one's emotion-memory) is fallacious, since personal experiences are either too weak to equate to the actions in the text, or on the other hand are so strong that they 'would dictate actions which have nothing to do with the play'.[17]

He attacks too the whole case for improvisation, on the grounds that improvisation can actually lead you into a false interpretation of what the writer is seeking to achieve.

Komisarjevsky adds the interesting conclusion that Stanislavsky was a better practitioner as both actor and director than he was a theorist, and that when he came to analyse and write down 'what he had discovered intuitively, he misinterpreted himself'.

The central feature of Stanislavsky's thinking seems to me, though, to be excellent good sense; you must relate to the text as fully as you possibly can if you are to make anything out of it. You may reject some of the ways which Stanislavsky proposes, but you have still to do the same thing: relate the play to yourself. As you forge the links, so your imagination is sparked off. Increasingly in education, quite apart from the theatre, it is the forging of such links that occupies the attention of teachers of literature and of drama. What does this text do to you? What is its impact on you? How do you feel about it? Indeed Stanislavsky is fully in line with Suzanne Langer and with modern educationists in his insistence that a work of art does nothing until it does something to you personally. It is your personal response, and its exploration and development, that actually matters.

In an interesting television interview some years ago, Albert Finney explained good-naturedly that he was not at all sorry that during his days as a student at the Royal Academy of Dramatic Art there had been no classes in improvisation or in any specific theory of acting. But he then went on to explain how, in preparing for John Osborne's *Luther* he found much inspiration from Erik Erikson's biography of the man; a classic instance of an actor employing one of Stanislavsky's main principles, that you must find out all you can about the subject-matter of the text. And indeed, in the same interview Finney described how as a boy at school he had prepared for a production of *Emperor Jones*:

> 'I remember going down to the docks in Salford . . . and studying the negro seamen because of the way they walked . . . that's because I wanted to reproduce the kind of movement that they had . . . that was when I was about sixteen.'[18]

The theorist whose work I would place second in significance to that of Stanislavsky is Rudolf Laban. In one respect at least it is odd to include him at all, since as far as I know Laban did not write or work with actors primarily in mind. His concern was with movement and with its relationship to mental health and to personality. But like all thinkers of great originality, his influence has outstripped his own field of activity, and his followers have made and are making a profound influence on education and, to a lesser degree, on the training of actors. The followers have also very much divided up into separate and sometimes opposing camps. But if one can talk of the essence of Laban's thinking, it is along some such lines as these:

> Each person's way of moving is distinctively different yet has certain common denominators; specifically, every movement has attributes of weight, space, time and flow. The particular quality though, with which these attributes are expressed will be endlessly different with each individual person. A person's quality of movement will (a) considerably influence the person's behaviour and (b) will enormously influence the way he appears to other people. Thus the way people move very much affects and reflects the personality.

All this has extensive implications in both education and in the theatre. If Laban is right, then clearly if a person can be helped to extend the range and quality of his movement he will be thereby helped towards a happier, fuller and healthier personality and way of life. This clearly becomes a cause of concern in schools, and so quite rightly the followers of Laban have started to replace (though I would underline the word *started* in this sentence) the high priests of Swedish drill and mass exercises of a more or less military nature. For Laban is diametrically opposed to the idea of everyone being compelled to do the same physical exercise in the same way and at the same speed. Essentially work of the kind recommended by Laban consists of individuals exploring their own movement skills for themselves, of discovering their own potential. And it may be worth adding that the best practical work in Laban movement that I have seen has all been related to dance. Pupils and students have been encouraged to extend and explore the quality of their movement to the accompaniment of music, both individually and also within small teams. The music and the dance provide an imaginative stimulus which inspires the student to move more confidently, more richly. Likewise, the worst work in Laban movement that I have seen has been closer to a military exercise than to the whole spirit of Laban, and has involved the students in painful attempts to perform specific kinds of movement at specific signals and in specific ways. The result has been a series of grunts and groans and, I would imagine, the very kind of horror at the mere thought of physical exercise which Laban was so concerned to dispel.

Quite rightly, and inevitably, teachers have begun to see the significance of Laban's work as regards the theatre. For if movement is a key factor in the make-up of a personality, then obviously the range of an actor's movement will enormously affect the range of the actor as such. Hence the absorption of large numbers of Laban-trained teachers into drama schools. Their work, though, is to be judged not by their attachment to the name of Laban, but by its results. If they help the student to achieve greater physical confidence, then they are doing well. If instead of liberating him they inhibit and depress him, they are making a poor job of their chosen task. They should, too, be able to demonstrate their significance to the actor in training not only by giving classes in movement as such, but more important, by joining a team for an actual production, and by so doing, show their usefulness to the actor as he works. Unfortunately, team-work among the staffs of drama academies is no more popular than it is in schools and colleges elsewhere.

If you have no experience of Laban's work it may be possible to join a Laban class. If you can, I warmly advise you to go along and have a look, and better still, to have a go. Reading his books is of limited value because of the very nature of the subject-matter.

Laban seems to be the one person who has attempted to study systematically what movement is, and what is its significance to the individual. I suspect that the value of his work will become much more widely recognised and explored over the next few decades.

I should like, too, to mention briefly another theorist, the German writer and director Bertolt Brecht. It could be said that whereas Stanislavsky is concerned with the actor's imagination, Brecht is concerned with the actor's projection, and that he sought to define the term in a very special way, which he termed the *alienation effect*:

'. . . the actor has to be clearly detached from his character. . . . There's no alienation effect when the actor adopts another's facial expression at the cost of erasing his own. What he should do is show the two faces overlapping . . .'[19]

And he gives as examples of this alienation the effect created when a small child plays an adult, or a man plays a woman.

The exact opposite of Brecht's alienation is usually intended in the theatre, though by no means always. Komisarjevsky, for instance, suggests that the actor must effectively disappear within the inner life of the character he is playing.[20] And he cites the case of Sarah Bernhardt who apparently was able at the age of eighty to play the part of a young girl so convincingly that the audience forgot they were watching the antiquated Bernhardt.

Why does Brecht argue the need for alienation?

The basis of his thinking is, of course, political: he seeks to change the political reality of the world through his theatre. Alienation is the main technique through which such change is to be achieved. Because the Brechtian actor stands outside the action, demonstrating that action to the audience, rather than getting carried away by it, so he also tells the audience to stand outside it, to think about it, and then to go out into the streets and change the world from what it is to what it could be. Brecht suggests that conventional, naturalistic acting blinds the audience into a sentimental involvement with the way things are, instead of opening their eyes to the possibility of change:

'If empathy makes something ordinary of a special event, alienation makes something special of an ordinary one. . . . The audience is no longer taking refuge from the present day in history; the present day becomes history.'

And:

'If the audience is to be shown how to handle the character, or if people who resemble it or are in similar situations are to be shown the secret of their problems, then he must adopt a standpoint which is not only outside the character's radius but also at a more advanced stage of evolution. The classics say that apes are best understood from the point of view of their successor in the evolutionary process, man . . .'

Perhaps the major criticism of Brechtian thinking is that in the theatre there always *is* alienation of one kind or another. All theatrical conventions alienate, and all experiments with and breaks with convention alienate also; they remind us that we are in a theatre, and that what we are watching is not actually happening. Theatre has always been created from a fusion of the two: of alienation (consciously watching a make-believe) and empathy (entering into the make-believe on an imaginative level). Idioms such as revue, music hall, burlesque, satire, farce, pantomime most obviously rely on alienation, on a capacity to distance oneself (whether actor or audience) from the action. And in a different way, this is true too of serious drama; we cannot respond fully to, say, *King Lear* or *Hamlet*, without thinking a great deal about what is happening and why, and whether it is right and just. And by so doing, we alienate ourselves from the drama. There is thus an ebb and flow in all audience response.

It may be worth adding, too, that when I saw Brecht's own company, the Berliner Ensemble, perform his masterpiece *Mother Courage* in London in 1956, there was no question that most of us in the audience were very deeply moved. Nor, with the best will in the world, can I say that I was remotely aware that the actors were playing themselves as well as the characters, other than in the basic sense that I am always aware in the theatre that I am in the theatre!

I suspect, then, that alienation is a basic feature of all acting, and that the actor, rather than needing to find ways to alienate must seek out the character he is playing within the context of the style and form of the play itself. Whether or not the audience will then leave the theatre and change the world, will depend on the audience, the play and the world. Nor is this intended in any way to mock the idea of a politically committed theatre, or conversely, to mock the idea of theatre that is politically uncommitted.

Learning to act

So far I have briefly outlined the basic skills of the actor, and indicated aspects of the theories of three of the major influences on modern thinking about those skills. Finally, I would like to try briefly to put them together, the skills and the theories, to suggest some of the things that may be worth doing if one wishes to act, or better still, if one wishes to become better at doing it.

1   Observe other actors, carefully and sympathetically.

2   Gain as much experience as you can on the stage. Carry on acting! Such advice will seem laughable to the professional actor in the queue at the Employment Exchange or phoning up his agent and never getting beyond the girl on the switchboard. But it remains good advice for all that. In particular, try to extend your range. Do things you have not done before. And try not to begin your acting career with starring roles (always presuming, of course, that you get the chance to do so).

3   Study the component skills of the actor's work, movement, voice and speech. Perhaps attend classes in Laban movement; also classes in voice and speech. Better still, find a good singing teacher, for he or she is more likely, in my own experience, to be able to teach you techniques of breath control than most speech teachers.

4   Extend your own knowledge, your own culture, as much as you can. Look sympathetically at cultures that are alien to you, at ideas you find difficult, at people you do not yet know.

5   Techniques and methods employed by individual actors may or may not be employed also by the director working with the company at rehearsal. It is up to the actor to supplement the director's method with his own method, to explore all the possible ways in which his skill and imagination can be employed to create a good performance. Perhaps the one attribute that most distinguishes the good actor, whether professional or amateur, is the extent to which he is able to work on his own at home, and so to bring to the next rehearsal something which was not there the day before.

This is related, too, to something which is often underestimated if not entirely ignored: the capacity to take time, to give oneself the chance to let the play and the production work for you, as the rehearsals gather momentum and the production takes shape. Constance Cummings expressed this well when talking of the rehearsals for the National Theatre production of *The Cherry Orchard*:

'When you start on it you feel isolated, and you feel the sentences are isolated. And then if you just go on and gently float down the river, it's almost as if Chekov was speaking to you and saying, "This is what I meant, and this is what relates back to that." It's very delicate. Then it seems to gather momentum, and you don't even think about whether you're lost.'[21]

6   There are as many different techniques of acting as there are actors, but they all seem to me to have two things in common: *effort* and *economy*. Considerable effort is needed to do any one of the many activities involved in acting: learning lines; working at rehearsal; studying the part and the play; overcoming one's nerves, daring to go on stage before an audience; sustaining a performance even when it seems to be going wrong, or when one has received a bad press. I should add that equal effort is involved in projecting one's voice and the rest of one's performance to the audience, and that if you do not consciously make such an effort it is unlikely that you are in fact projecting. Economy is involved, in that the actor, like any artist, is asking the audience to attend and respond to certain things, and all attention and response involve an element of selection. The less an actor does, the more the audience will attend to those things which he wishes them to attend to.

4 Improvised Productions

We can distinguish a number of ways in which a production may be improvised:

1   The text may be improvised by the actors and director at rehearsal, without any written dialogue being given to the actors in the first instance. By the time of performance the text may be fixed, more or less, and will incorporate many of the ideas that have evolved through improvisation.

2   The play may be improvised, more or less from scratch, at performance.

3   The company may start with a written text, and be encouraged to improvise with this throughout the period of rehearsal and, perhaps, to rewrite it. They then perform it in this new and improvised form.

4   The company may take a theme and then do research into the theme and improvise a form of revue around it. There may be incorporated into the work a certain amount of script that is written by members of the company independently of improvisation.

5   The company may devise a drama in front of the audience, but the improvisation is structured before they start. I discuss this later in the chapter.

The idea of improvisation

The word 'improvisation' has come to arouse such controversy in both theatre and education (with some shrinking away in horror at the mere mention of the word, and others waxing lyrical at the very thought of it) that it may be worth briefly talking about what an improvisation is, and why its use has been so strongly advocated.

When we speak of actors improvising a drama we generally mean a group rather than a solitary activity. It is, of course, perfectly possible for one person to improvise a drama on his own; acting in his own room, perhaps using the tape recorder, and playing just one character or more than one character. And the writer who works out his script is also improvising, and similarly, every performance of every written script involves an element of improvisation on the actor's part. But generally speaking, when we talk of improvised drama, we mean people getting together to create drama of some kind without a written text to tell them exactly what must be said or done next. In most forms of improvisation there will be various starting points and various rules which in one way or another will limit the total freedom of the improvisers. For instance, the basic situation will be agreed on, perhaps in considerable detail (as in structured improvisation). There will be the basic moral rule underlying all drama: that it is *make-believe*, not reality, and that whatever is done will be *imaginary*; thus if you improvise a fight, you will not actually hurt the other person. Improvisers may also very reasonably want to add other rules: that certain situations must be avoided in the drama, perhaps. The working out of these rules may be essential preliminaries to successful improvisation. Like all group activities, an improvisation can only work where people get along well, trust each other and believe in the value of what they are doing.

Why improvise?

While the roots of improvisation (in drama) stretch right back into history, it is fair to say that modern interest in it dates back to two sources of influence, both of them of the twentieth century: Stanislavsky and Moreno.

I outlined briefly the work of Stanislavsky in the chapter on acting. He explored the use of improvisation in two major ways: as a way of helping the actor to understand what a text is actually doing and saying, and also as a way of helping him to relate that text to his own experience of life.

J. L. Moreno is an Austrian-American who, in the 1930s and 1940s did a great deal of work exploring the uses of improvisation as a way of helping people's social and emotional development, and especially in the treatment of the neurotic and the delinquent.[22] Moreno summed up his thinking in his massive work *Who Shall Survive?* in which his basic argument is that the cure for the unhappiness and neurosis of our time lies in a massive extension of creative opportunities, and that these opportunities need to be opportunities to create *with others*. He suggests that western culture places too much emphasis upon people creating things *on their own*, and that it follows this up by demanding that we also respond to such creativity *on our own*. In other words, says Moreno, the creativity of our culture largely consists of X writing, say, a novel, and of Y and Z reading it in solitary state. Likewise the theatre consists of X writing a play, which is then given to A and B and C to act, thereby reducing them to puppets, and then offered to D, E and F (the public) who are expected to respond with no more animation than a corpse who somehow is able to clap at the end.

It is far more important, Moreno says, that people should get together to create their own drama. Only in this way can we achieve greater spontaneity. Fixed scripts performed by actors to an audience simply perpetuate the decadence of the society; they do not give opportunities to the audience (or even the actors) to act out for themselves their own ideas, their own problems. They perpetuate, too, a cultural hierarchy where the best is equated with the finished, the completed (and therefore the dead), such as the works of Shakespeare, instead of being equated with the creativity, the spontaneity, of each and every one of us. Life is something we do with one another. Life is social. And the road to a fully creative, spontaneous life is through all those situations where we are given the chance to create, to be spontaneous, *together*. And thus the supreme importance of improvised drama.

Moreno deplored the work of Stanislavsky, because the latter seemed to him to use improvisation for exactly the wrong purpose. Stanislavsky relegates improvisation to the status of a tool in the service of a written text, whereas Moreno would do away with the written text altogether. Nobody's script, not even Shakespeare's, is as good as the script the actor creates for himself with other actors. It is the here and now that counts. Not what somebody wrote down yesterday or last year. Culture means creating, not interpreting, analysing, responding (though it will include these). And a culture disintegrates at the point where it elevates the creative work of others (dead or alive) over and above your own creativity. As a sequel to such disintegration, or as a symptom of it, vast numbers of people will believe that they are not creative (and hence not alive) and turn to the creativity not so much of geniuses but of hacks and second-raters. They will watch mediocre material on television and the like, when they could in fact create better material themselves, and indeed could not fail to create better material.

Despite the extravagance of Moreno's thinking, its central proposition is close to the heart of all progressive thinking in modern education (A. S. Neill, John Holt, John Dewey included): that the most learning takes place when you are given the chance to create for yourself, to find out for yourself, to test your own ideas against other people's. And improvisation can rightly be seen as one of the ways (though not necessarily the only way) in which creativity can be explored through drama and theatre.

All of which brings us to the central question: does improvisation belong to the theatre – or to education – or to both?

Before trying to answer this question, Moreno is helpful in clarifying what happens when people improvise. He suggests that all improvisation tends towards one of two kinds, and he calls these *psycho-drama* and *socio-drama*.

A psycho-drama occurs where the improvisers are at the service of the director (who may also be a fellow-actor) and he tells them what to do. This mode of improvisation may be deliberately set up as such, in a therapeutic context, say, where the patient becomes the director, and the therapist believes that by giving him the chance to enact, or to see enacted, his particular fantasies the patient may overcome his sickness or neurosis. The actors are in effect nurses, assistants to the therapist-doctor (and presumably they have the rights of a nurse not to be injured in any way by the patient). But an improvisation can become a psycho-drama without being deliberately set up as such, for it may be taken over in midstream by a dominant personality who reduces everyone else to subservience. And a great deal of cinema may in fact be the psychodrama of the director, as he manipulates actor and script in the service of his own imagination, to act out his own fantasies. This will less commonly be true of the theatre since so much will be scripted before the actors come together, but it could be true of a certain amount of improvised theatre, where the actors' improvisations have taken place under the control of the director.

The other kind of improvisation is socio-drama, where all the participants have equal rights (even though they may be working on an idea that emanates from one or other of them, or from someone else). All the participants have therefore equal opportunities to be spontaneous. No one is in command. It gives greater opportunities to everyone. Each can explore, each can respond. We can try out a great variety of roles, a great variety of situations. With such imaginative experience behind us we will go on to live the more richly, for we have extended our experience – but in a make-believe context where we can learn from our mistakes and play more roles than we have in fact yet played in real life.

Generally speaking, when we set up an improvisation, whether in the theatre or in education, we are setting out to create a socio-drama where all will contribute equally. Very often, though, the drama becomes monopolised by one person and it may then become a psycho-drama, with the rest more or less taking their cues entirely from this one person. This may distress the director (in the theatre) or the teacher (in education) or it may delight him. This brings us on to the main question:

Does improvisation belong either to education or to the theatre?

First, what is the educational value of improvisation? Why should it be included in the school curriculum? In brief, my answer is that it extends people's understanding of each other, and their capacity to work with each other. The group of young-sters, for instance, who improvise a scene together around an imaginary breakfast table with an imaginary set of family characters, teach each other an enormous amount about the world they come from, their attitudes, their language, their ex-perience. Such teaching is couched, of course, not in explicit information so much as in jokes, in irony and in all the various twists of the drama. One might say that improvisation allows the improvisers, and their audience if there is one, to share each other's world view in the context of make-believe, and that very often the improvisation takes the form of a joke that is devised and worked out together. It is this 'togetherness' which is also important. Evolving the idea, acting it out together, can be an enormously satisfying experience. When an improvisation really works it is as if the whole is greater than the sum of its separate parts, as if the group has achieved something which no one member of the group could have achieved on his or her own. When the group reach this stage they have not only learnt something from the improvisation itself, but also have learnt a great deal simply about working with each other. They are likely to be better at working together than they were previously. To return to Moreno's terminology, when a group reach the point where they can create socio-dramas, and are no longer being diverted into unwitting psycho-dramas at the dictates of a parti-cularly aggressive or disturbed member of the group, then they have all matured enormously as human beings.

The difficulty lies in getting the group to the stage of socio-drama, to the point where the members can all contribute equally to the improvisation without any one member sub-jugating the others. (There then remains the further difficulty of distinguishing subjugation from inspiration, for the im-proviser who seems to one person simply to force himself on to the others, to dominate, may seem to another to be the in-spiring source of the group's ideas.) And in education this difficulty is felt not only by the group but also by the person responsible for the group: the teacher. In other words, what is the teacher's job when the class split up into groups and start to improvise? What does the teacher have to do? Sit back, watch and enjoy himself?

Fundamentally, the teacher's task is to follow Stanislavsky's precept, and train the pupil/student to ask: IF. . . . If this person does that, what might happen next? If there are two obvious possibilities, is there a third, perhaps less obvious? If this happened to me, what would I do? And what might people other than myself have done? What are the possibilities? The teacher can encourage his class to practise this precept in two basically different ways, and he will probably use both ways a great deal: he can stand outside the improvisation and, through various questions and suggestions, help the group to improvise more successfully, or he will step into the improvisation and actually assume a character. In time, the whole class will instinctively pick up the same skill the teacher is practising, and will throw out questions and assume characters not only to help their own groups but also to help other groups whose work they are watching.

The teacher, though, has to achieve a delicate balance. His interventions must not so dominate the proceedings that the whole thing becomes an elaborate psycho-drama of which the principal beneficiary is himself. In particular, he must not be so keen on a particular kind of finished product that he effectively denies the group or the class the chance to grow towards a standard of their own, and equally important, the chance to work their way through their own particular psycho-dramas while on their way to better things. Much can be achieved through a sympathetic study of what children actually do when they improvise, through looking carefully at their ideas, their jokes, their language. Just as the best developments in the teaching of art have emanated from an interest in the work of the child, as opposed to a concern that all children should be able to draw and paint the same things in the same ways, so the best work in improvised drama is achieved where the teacher can balance his own imagination, his own dramatic skill, his own judgment, with a capacity to let children achieve their own standards for themselves.

And this brings us to the second half of the question: does improvisation have a valid place in the theatre as an art-form which the actor may present to the audience? Or is it exclusively a type of dramatic exercise which helps the actor at rehearsal but has little if anything to offer to an audience? The number of productions in recent years which have involved a large element of improvisation and which made very compelling theatre, indicate that improvised drama can work brilliantly, that audiences can respond to it with great excitement. Works such as *Oh What a Lovely War*, *Us* and *Hang Down Your Head and Die*, are some of the classic demonstrations of this. Nor does this mean that actors will not have basically the same problems when they come to improvise as children have when they do their improvisations in the classroom. For a group of people to evolve a production is difficult enough in any event; to do so without a written text to work from, is bound to be even harder. This does not mean that an improvised production is intrinsically better than a pre-scripted one (though, of course, Moreno would argue otherwise). Everything will depend on the impact the production makes on the audience.

The scope for improvised productions is very considerable, and they offer opportunities for a company to work and experiment together, to get to know their own and each other's potential, to an extent that may be denied by a scripted play. And so I devote the final sections of the chapter to a discussion of two kinds of improvised production and the ways in which they may be undertaken: improvised productions based on a theme (I use as an example a show in which I was myself involved) and structured improvisation.

Before moving on to these, I would like to add to the discussion on the theatrical versus the educational value of improvisation, by suggesting that the *versus* is misleading. Whatever makes good theatre is also highly educational. A good play. A good production. Working on a good production. Seeing a good production. There is no antithesis between theatre and education. Similarly, a good drama school offers its actors-in-training an education that can compare with any offered at a university or college. Seeing good theatre, and making it — both are important parts of our culture, and we are educated by both of them.

Improvised productions based on a theme

What follows is simply an illustration of one such production, which I directed at Thomas Huxley College, a college for the training of mature students as teachers. None of the students involved in the production was a drama specialist. They were all specialising in a great variety of other subjects, but all of them (roughly fifty in number) expressed interest in working with me on a production. We worked together on a completely extra-curricular basis, in our own time, and were joined by several members of staff.

1   The career of Mata Hari, the dancing lady who was shot by the French in 1917 for spying for the Germans, has long intrigued me. After doing a modest amount of research into her life, I became convinced of her innocence, and equally sure that the circumstances leading up to her execution were bizarre and frightening. The possibility of doing an improvised show, using her life as the theme, seemed very promising.

2   I suggested a basic framework to the company within which we could at once start to improvise and research. Act One would be devoted to the *legend* of Mata Hari, Act Two to the probable *reality* of her life. Act One would evoke the Mata Hari of the cinema, as portrayed by Jeanne Moreau, Greta Garbo and others, and by the many novels and memoirs in which she has figured. Act Two would attempt to piece together some kind of probable truth. Both acts would follow the same main sequence: both would begin at the outbreak of War, with Mata Hari in Berlin; both would show her visit to France, her later visit to Madrid, and then her return to France, her trial and execution. But while the second act would repeat the basic outline of the first, it would show an entirely different portrait of what actually happened.

3   Many members of the company did research into the legend and the reality of Mata Hari through reading the various published biographies, accounts of the activities of other spies and accounts of the War itself. Although we were unfortunately unable to hire any of the Mata Hari films, some of the company succeeded in seeing the Greta Garbo film when it made a brief visit to a London cinema. We were also able to hire a most interesting film of newsreel compilations, showing Paris in the years leading up to the Great War, the period of Mata Hari's success as a dancer. We did some work at the newspaper library of the British Museum, and we assembled a collection of photos of Mata Hari and of the world she lived in.

4   Working within the framework which I had devised at the outset, we improvised various scenes for both versions of Mata Hari's progress to the execution squad, along roughly these lines:

Scene 1   *the legend* (Act 1)
Mata Hari dancing and living riotously in Berlin, while training as a German spy.

Scene 2   She comes back to France in the early stages of

Scene 1   *the reality* (Act 2)
Mata Hari stranded in Berlin at the outset of War, with no money, and her career a shambles.

2   She begs and borrows her journey back to France,

the War, and at once starts spying (while also dancing very successfully).

Scene 3   She is sent by the Germans to Madrid, which is neutral and a hive of international activity. She regrets only that she must leave her latest lover.

Scene 4   She has numerous affairs in Madrid, and relays information from French lovers (about army manoeuvres, etc) to German lovers.

Scene 5   She returns to Paris to resume her dancing career, stars at the Folies Bergères, and is arrested for espionage as she walks off the stage from her greatest artistic triumph.

Scene 6   Trial: Mata Hari proud and splendid as the brutal truth is hurled at her.

Scene 7   Execution: she dances and reminisces in her prison cell, and goes off to the firing squad with all the panache of a leading lady.

and sponges off friends and lovers.

3   She meets an old acquaintance who, she discovers, works for French intelligence. She offers her services as a spy. The French send her to Madrid.

4   She becomes involved with a complex network of German and French double-agents, fails to understand what is happening and learns nothing whatever.

5   She returns to Paris, penniless and confused. Her employers in the secret service disown her and disclaim her, denying all knowledge of her activities. Possibly in order to create a scapegoat and to distract public attention from the defeats of the War, the government charge her with espionage.

6   Trial: Mata Hari utterly defeated and confused as the alleged facts are hurled at her.

7   Execution: still entirely confused and frightened, she is executed.

Some of the improvisations we 'structured' (I give an example below) while others were freely improvised around the situations; ie we agreed roughly on what would happen in the scene, took different characters, and then tried to dramatise. Sometimes we recorded the improvisations on tape recorders — never very successfully or usefully, because the tape got in the way of the work. We usually worked independently in small groups and then brought back our improvisations to show to each other. The best part of all this activity was the talk which followed. Good ideas were often created out of improvisations which as a whole did not achieve very much, but this was part of the exercise: to exploit all the different ways in which different people can pool their resources. These ideas were then incorporated into the growing body of material.

5   As we improvised, so we also started to fix the script, however tentatively. Once we felt we had something worth keeping we would endeavour to get the scene on to paper. We did not necessarily keep the scene in this format for the rest of the production, but it did give us a feeling that the whole thing was building up. Some of us were better at writing the scenes down than others, just as some were better at improvising than others. In the business of assembling a final script, I incorporated some scenes which an individual had written in this way (after improvisations), alongside some scenes which I pieced together from different versions written by different people, together with some scenes written entirely by myself. We rehearsed twice a week for roughly five months, and we spent the first half of this period improvising and the second half rehearsing the finished script. This finished script went through many changes as we talked further about what the drama was about, what the characters were doing, and the sort of people they were. I would say that the talk that occurred among all of us at rehearsal about (a) the improvisations and (b) the final text, was the most interesting and fruitful aspects of the whole project.

6   We wanted the first half, the legend, to be as colourful and preposterous as a Hollywood romantic epic, so we included as many varied modes of entertainment as we could. We started the play with a filmed sequence of Mata Hari dancing, which one of the students made with a very cheap camera and without a soundtrack. We later added a soundtrack for the performance, where we faded from the filmed image of Mata Hari into the same actress playing Mata Hari live. We also wanted plenty of singing and dancing. Two members of the company wrote a song about Mata Hari, which we had people singing all over Europe wherever she went. And the pianist wrote a romantic love theme which we used as accompaniment to all her various romantic encounters. The actor who played her lover was also a folk dancer (Russian) so we made the character a Russian prince who, having fallen on hard times, has joined a dancing troupe, and he happens to be dancing rather splendidly in a cabaret show when he meets Mata Hari. (In the second act, the reality, he became just a gigolo fallen on hard times.) Another player had a good singing voice, so we incorporated a brief sequence into Mata Hari's arrival in Madrid, where a famous opera star happens to be staying in the same hotel and entertains the guests with an excerpt from Lehar.

7 For our research into the reality for the second act we got one of our historians to give us a breakdown of the major events of the War, so that we could fit Mata Hari's career into the actual happenings in the world outside. We wanted to include a sequence where she visits her lover before going off to Madrid — he has joined the French Air Force by this time — but we did not want a long verbal sequence. One of the company was an expert photographer, so she took a series of photographs of Mata Hari and her lover to represent their short time together, and we then did the scene as a sequence of photos flashed (very large) on to the cyclorama, and with a very brief taped dialogue going through it together with theme music. It was very effective.

8 Our one real disaster was the costumes. A group of students produced some excellent costume designs, and then proceeded to make the costumes with very little cash and with very cheap materials. As a result they all looked exactly that — cheap! So we scrapped the whole lot and everyone somehow found and adapted clothes from their own and their friends' wardrobes which were right for the play. We also hired some military costumes for the men.

9 I encouraged individual members of the company to experiment in directing individual scenes, but I myself retained control over the production as a whole. Small groups took control of lighting (designing and operating), of front-of-house, and of scenery and staging. The scenery was modest: a couple of painted flats to help evoke something of the atmosphere in a non-representational way.

10 We staged the show in a small lecture theatre which had only one door, so we kept the actors on stage throughout (ie we had them sit down on either side of the stage when they were not acting). We regrouped the stage rostra to make an entirely different stage for the second half: we wanted the first act to be wide open and epic in style — an extravaganza; while we wanted the second act to be more claustrophobic and limited in movement. Mata Hari was no longer dancing across Europe like a great star, but virtually limping from one place to the next. So we kept a clear space for the first half, with the rostra on either side, and then brought the rostra right into the centre of the stage-area for the second half.

11 I cast the main roles at the beginning of the production, and then cast other parts as we progressed. The basic idea I worked on was that Mata Hari would be played by a different actress in each act (both of them excellent actresses, by the way), while all the other characters would be played by the same actors in each act. This meant that the audience could identify the events of the second half by the actors involved,

even though the psychology and the significance of these events was now quite different.

So the production involved a fair variety of people working together and doing a fair variety of different things. Not all of these different things are peculiar to an improvised production, but it may even so be useful to try to spell them out. They included:

improvising dialogue
writing scenes
discussing ideas — for possible scenes, for scenes being improvised, for scenes being written, discussing ideas for the play as such throughout all the stages of production
research of various kinds
writing music
writing lyrics
choreographing dance sequences
directing scenes
dancing, singing, acting
film-making
photography
taping soundtracks
costume design and making
designing and operating a lighting plot
stage management, and front-of-house
scenic design, and making of scenery
designing and making programmes
joining in the production as occasional or regular visitors to rehearsals, not as intending actors but simply as people interested in the production, and taking part as members of a seminar, making suggestions and contributing to the dialogue.

Two points may be worth making in conclusion: first, that many members of the company did much more than one of the things I have listed, while others did only one. And some withdrew in the course of rehearsal, not in a sulk, and not slamming the door behind them, but simply because the production took longer than we had expected and they were not able to sustain the tax on their free time. We originally planned to do the production in nine weeks, but we took twice as long as this. And we could have gone on longer. But there is an optimum time in such ventures, and I think we could not have gone on any longer without disintegrating as a group. I may add that only half a dozen people had to withdraw. The second point is that an activity like this gives people an opportunity to learn about all manner of things, even though they do not necessarily do these things themselves in the production. They see the growth of an idea from a single sheet of information outlining a framework, into a complex two-hour production involving some fifty people. They see actors evolving a characterisation; lighting plots being devised and tried out; costumes being made; all manner of skills being brought together. And this opportunity not only to do the very thing which you are yourself contributing, but also to see how other people make their contributions, and to learn from what you see, seems to me to be a basic part of the richness of experience which any good production offers to all those who are involved in it.

Structured improvisation

The kind of production which I have just discussed consists largely of material that has been improvised *before* performance. Of productions which are improvised *in front of* the audience, I would distinguish two main kinds: free improvisation, and structured improvisation. Free improvisation will include working to some given stimulus, such as a news story, a situation, specific kinds of character, etc.

The idea of a *structured* improvisation is as follows:

1 The director sets up the improvisation in considerable detail. He writes out beforehand the instructions for each character, and creates a full structure for the drama.

2 The improvisation takes place in front of the audience; this kind of work is ideal for small audiences, such as you would have in a classroom or seminar. The director reads out the instructions to each character in front of the audience, but with the other characters outside the room.

3 Once each character has been instructed, they all get together and improvise the scene. The actors know only their own instructions. The audience know everybody's. For all concerned it can be a fascinating exercise, and one of the incidental services it can provide is to demonstrate how complex an action can become: how long it may take for the major action to surface, and how often it can be defeated by other things suddenly happening.

4 The art of devising such an improvisation seems to be to provide the characters with a clear line of action on more than one level at once, ie with something to do immediately (such as borrow a fiver) and something more fundamental to attempt to achieve (such as buy a motor-car to impress the girl-friend). In Stanislavsky terms, provide a sub-text as well as a text.

5 It helps enormously to provide as much in the way of props

and furnishings as you possibly can, facilities for making tea, for instance, or at least an actual cup (or cups) of tea.

6   The director must be able to answer questions from each character prior to the improvisation which he may want to raise before starting.

7   After the improvisation there will be much discussion between the actors and the audience and the director. This is probably the most interesting part of the activity. What did we expect to happen, in contrast with what did? What got lost? Why? How?

The idea of structured improvisation is an extremely exciting one. I give below a couple of examples. But the possibilities are infinite, and I hope you will be interested to experiment for yourself. The first example I devised while the company were working on the theme of *Mata Hari*. The second I devised for an early rehearsal for a dramatisation of Stendhal's novel *The Scarlet and the Black*.

1   *For three characters*
   Margaret, an actress in her early forties
   Ann, her friend, also an actress, about thirty
   Tony, Margaret's lover, about thirty

Instructions for all three characters
The three of you are living in Margaret's small flat in London (in Bayswater) and have been living there for some months. To be precise the flat is rented by Margaret, and Ann shares the flat with her whenever she is out of work and/or living in London. When Ann is there she pays Margaret half of the rent. Tony has been living there since he and Margaret fell in love, about ten weeks ago, when they met at a party. There are three rooms in the flat, so each of you has a space you can more or less call your own. The biggest room is Margaret's, which you also use as a kind of sitting room, and which leads into the kitchen. It is in this room that the scene takes place. *Margaret* is an actress who achieved sudden fame twenty years ago in a series of comedy films which attempted to set her up as a kind of English version of Brigitte Bardot. For a while the films had quite a popularity, and Margaret became a star, earning a lot of money — £20000 a year, for about four years. But the tax man came and took away some of it, and all of the rest Margaret either gave away to friends, or spent, and ever since then (for the past fifteen years or so) the going has been rough. From time to time she appears in films, very occasionally, and in very small parts as bartenders and landladies. But she often meets up with old friends from her heyday, and they inspire her to dream of a sensational come-back to stardom. In the meantime the debts

accumulate, and the occasional performance arranged by Margaret's theatrical agent only just manages to keep her head above water. But she will not for one moment tolerate the thought of earning a living other than as an actress. *Ann* has not yet had much success, but she has done some good work for repertory companies, and in small parts on television and on film. Many think her a very clever actress who will one day be a great success. She met Margaret when both were working briefly on a film, and they have been friends ever since. *Tony* has had a career as a dancer in the chorus of several West End musicals, but at the moment he is out of work, and has been so for quite a long time. He has had an adventurous life, having run away from home when he was fifteen and joined the Merchant Navy and seen the world.

The scene begins with Ann and Tony at home, and in a few moments Margaret returns from a day out shopping.

Instructions for Margaret

These are difficult times for you. Not only is there very little work, and therefore very little money, but your emotional life is hard also. You are very much in love with Tony, but you suspect, perhaps wrongly, perhaps foolishly, that Ann is falling in love with him also. Various intuitions on your part indicate this to you, but you have no precise evidence. You are confident of Tony's love for you, but you also know that he is a very easy, very adaptable person, who could be misled by someone such as Ann into making a fool of himself. So even though you like Ann very much (though you know she is not good enough to make the grade as an actress) you are desperate to find some money so that you can afford to ask Ann to go and live else-where — and also so that you can afford a few luxuries for Tony, who has no money and cannot find work. Today, you've been unexpectedly lucky. You were on your way to visit your agent, when you met an old friend, Bill Robbins, whom you hardly recognised, and who took you out for a very expensive lunch. Bill is a business man of some sort, and in the course of the conversation he said he could arrange for you to do some very interesting work. It would involve a tour of American night clubs, in which you would sing and dance and maybe re-enact some excerpts from your old films. You asked if Tony could come also, and he agreed. Perhaps Tony will sing and dance in the show with you. He offered you an advance fee of £1000 (to be paid tomorrow, when you would call in to his office to sign a con-tract) and a further £500 for every town you played in America. The only stipulation he made was an odd one: that either he or his colleagues would look after your luggage (including its packing). You readily agreed to his offer, even though you suspect that Bill Robbins is a bit of a crook, and who knows, there might be some tie-up with drugs or something like that. But that's no business of yours. You're an artist. But there is one snag: Ann knows Bill Robbins also, and if you mention his name to her she will immediately pour scorn over the whole idea, and maybe discourage Tony from coming with you. So in talking about it, you will not mention Bill at all, but simply find a false name for the 'impresario' who finances the tour. So when you get home you will have several objectives: to inspire Tony with thoughts of a three-month tour of the States, perhaps appearing with you, perhaps just coming along for the fun of it and to be together; and to persuade Ann to move out of the flat so that you can spend the next four weeks, prior to the tour, with the flat to yourselves.

Instructions for Ann and Tony (together)

Tony has decided to move out. He's tired of Margaret, and equally tired of her lack of money and her abundance of imagination. She goes on endlessly about the famous people she has known, the famous people who are going to help her, and the money she will have tomorrow (but never today). Also Tony has fallen in love with a younger woman with whom he is going to live for a while. This he has told Ann in the course of the day, and she can see no sense in trying to stop him from going. Both know that Margaret will be upset, but Tony takes the view that she must cope with her disappointment, and that's that. Ann and Tony have an agreeable relationship with one another, and Ann does not blame him for the kind of unhappiness which she knows he will now cause Margaret. She regards Margaret as the kind of person who can't help getting involved when she shouldn't – and that's part of Margaret's charm. Earlier in the day, just after Margaret had left the flat a fellow by the name of Bill Robbins phoned and wanted to speak to Margaret. Ann told him that she was out shopping and might perhaps be visiting her agent also. After putting down the phone, Ann remembered that Robbins is someone she met a long time ago, and that he is quite definitely a crook of some kind, indeed some reckon he's something to do with an international racket in dope-peddling. You make a mental note to warn Margaret to have nothing to do with him if he phones again.

For Ann (alone)

The present period of time out of work has deeply depressed you, and the occasional odd job as a shop assistant, etc, does nothing to cheer you up, even though it does bring in a bit of necessary cash. After a great deal of thinking about it, you have decided to change your career, to give up acting and to train as a nurse. You're not quite sure how to go about it, but when you go home to your parents at the weekend (in Bristol) you will have a chat with them about it and also with a friend who is a nurse. Your parents will be delighted. Nursing will be a deeply useful way of spending your life, and will keep you very fully and happily occupied, even though it will also be hard work. You have not yet told Margaret. You know she thinks highly of you as an actress, and will be very disappointed. But you must make up your mind and keep to it, despite the fact that it may be difficult, for a while at least, to cope with the knowledge that your theatre days are over.

For Tony (alone)
You have not had a steady job since leaving the Merchant Navy ten years ago, nor have you ever graced the stage of any theatre anywhere; that is a gentle lie with which you have made Margaret happy. As far as you know you can neither sing nor dance nor act. You've lived always on your wits and your charm, and while this has never been easy nor has it ever been dull — except for the last couple of months with Margaret. But last week you answered an advert in *The Times* from a business-man looking for a chauffeur to drive him and his wife across Europe and back. You're a good driver, you made a good impression at the interview, and you got the job — even though your references were rather short, and left many gaps in your working career. The money's good, and you start this evening. But it does not suit you to tell Ann or Margaret that you are going off to be a chauffeur, so you have concocted this tale about a love affair with a younger woman; and if Margaret presses you for details, you'll just make them up or else refuse to tell her anything. Whichever you choose. You are now packing your things and almost ready to leave.

As the scene begins Ann is perhaps making tea/coffee, Margaret returns home a few moments after the scene begins.

2   *For three characters*
     Kate, aged eighteen
     Harry, her brother, aged twenty-one
     George, her father, aged about fifty

Instructions for all three characters
George is a highly successful businessman and Member of Parliament (Conservative). *Kate* is soon to go up to Oxford to study law. She is at present in the midst of her summer holidays after leaving school. *Harry*, after failing all his examinations at school, has spent the last three years or so travelling around Europe and America, and engaging not very successfully in various attempts to settle down. He is also an excellent athlete and is particularly good at boxing and fencing. Some months

ago Harry was introduced by his father to a gentleman named Andrews who runs a travel agency, and as a result of this meeting Harry spent a short time as Andrews' business partner. But Harry quickly tired of the business and left it, telling his father that he would rather set up business on his own. Their mother died some twelve years ago, when the children were quite small, and both Harry and Kate have spent most of their lives at boarding schools. Kate did brilliantly at school. All three get along well together: Harry seems quite to admire his clever young sister; Kate sees Harry as a charming ne'er-do-well; she sees her father as a clever but slightly dull person, out of touch with many of the most exciting modern ideas and thinking. Both the children have a handsome allowance from their father — £200 each, per month. Harry has been getting this allowance for the past few years, while Kate has only been getting it since she left school.

A few months ago George engaged a new private secretary, a young man named Edward Browne, who got the job thanks to the recommendation of an old friend of George's who tutors at a Cambridge college. It seems that Edward was a student at the college, and doing brilliantly, but he suddenly gave up his studies (History) because he found the strain too much to cope with. He was near, in fact, to a nervous breakdown. The tutor sympathised and helped him to find a job, and hearing that George was looking for a new secretary he suggested Edward to him. Edward has done well at the work, but at the moment he has gone home for a week to his parents in Newcastle. (His father is a bus conductor.) While he is working with George he sometimes stays at the house, but he also has a room of his own in a lodging house nearby.

At the beginning of the scene, which takes place in the drawing room of the family's London home, George is having a drink before going off to a parliamentary debate, and Kate joins him prior to going to the theatre with some old school-friends. And Harry is due home at any moment, having spent the day in a gymnasium, keeping fit.

Instructions for George

You have had lunch earlier today with the gentleman (Andrews) with whom you arranged for Harry to go into business. You had not seen him since Harry gave up the business. Andrews complained rather bitterly to you about Harry's behaviour while they were working together: he was always late for appointments, forgot matters of importance and even mislaid correspondence. Andrews also implied that Harry might have been actively dishonest, possibly even taking money that belonged not to him but to the firm. He refused though, to be precise about this. It is clear that Harry must find himself a decent occupation and make something of himself. He's seen the world, and he's cost you a great deal of money, and he must now start to take life seriously. You have a friend called Dick Maclean who owns a vast business in the making and selling of men's clothes, and he is looking for a smart young man of good background to assist in setting up an extension of the business in Australia. It would involve going out to Australia next week for a few months of preliminary work and activity. You know that Harry would be ideal. You phoned Maclean this afternoon, suggested Harry for the job, and Maclean has asked to meet Harry tomorrow morning for an interview. You are very hopeful for the whole idea. So you will make an all-out effort to get Harry to co-operate fully. If he does well in the Australian business, you could help him to start a business empire of his own. If Harry gets difficult, you may have to threaten to stop his monthly allowance, but you hope very much that you will not have to do this. If needs be, you can enlist Kate to help persuade her brother.

Instructions for Kate

The past month or so has been rendered remarkable for you by the presence of Edward, your father's new secretary, a young man whose views on life and society both correspond to and challenge your own. Unbeknown to your father and to anyone else you have had an affair with him, and fallen very deeply in love. Although he is superficially the perfect secretary, he fundamentally dislikes your father and everything he stands for, and you in your turn have come to question your father's values much more deeply than before. Edward has fallen in love with you, too, he says, and you believe him. Earlier today he phoned you from London airport to say that he is leaving his job, leaving you (most reluctantly) and leaving England. He intends to work his way around Europe and to find out about himself and the world — to find his own soul, in fact. Deeply distressed, you begged him not to go without you, and he eventually agreed that he would meet you at an address in Paris later this week. You have therefore had to make several important decisions very quickly. You love Edward above everything, and would rather abandon the chance of university and a career than lose him. You know your father would never support the idea of your marrying Edward, so you must act without him or anyone else knowing what you are doing. Your plan is this: you will go immediately to Paris, taking a flight later this evening, and pretending to your father that the friends with whom you were going to go to the theatre have cancelled their plans at short notice, and are going to Paris instead, and you are hoping to go with them. You will ask him for say, £200 or £300, or more if he proves amenable, to allow you to live comfortably with Edward for a few weeks or more. You will write to your father from Paris later on, to explain that you have decided to postpone your entry to university for a year or two, in order to enable you to study in France. He will then continue to give you your monthly allowance, and this will permit you to live fairly comfortably with Edward, though either or both of you will no doubt take various occasional jobs as bartenders and the like. You will marry Edward, but you will not tell your father about this, nor will you ever mention Edward's name in your letters, until some time in the future when you think it will be possible for Edward to be 'accepted' into the family.

Obviously your father will not now be able to let you have a lot of money in cash, but he could give you a cheque which you could then cash at the airport.

The important thing is this: that no one should know what is happening; that you should take as much money to France as possible; and that your father's great wealth should continue to flow in your (and Edward's) direction for the rest of your lives. To avoid all possible suspicion, you will arrange with Edward that he never lets it be known that he has gone to the continent at all, least of all to France.

This is the first time you have ever been in love.

Instructions for Harry

You've had a good day at the gymnasium, and are very much looking forward to an international fencing contest which will be taking place in London the month after next and where you will be a member of the British team; or at least you will be if you get through the selection trials which are to be held tomorrow. And everyone expects you to be selected. When the contest is over, you seriously intend to turn over a new leaf and find yourself some kind of business to settle into. You might even have a go at politics, though you have no idea how you would actually do that — no doubt father could give you some tips. Also, of course, you have hopes of falling in love some time and getting married. You think you may even be falling in love with the sister of an old school-friend, Caroline, a delightful girl who refuses to take you seriously, on the grounds that you have no permanent occupation. Her father is a very rich solicitor. You're not absolutely sure that you're in love with her, and you're positive that you're not besotted with her in the way that your sister Kate is quite clearly besotted with Edward, the new secretary. You're rather suspicious of that young man. Is he dependable? Is he a gentleman? But your father does not seem to be at all aware of what is going on — the two of them are clearly having an affair, and Kate is acting really quite strangely. A girl of her age would be capable of doing something really stupid and disastrous for the love of such a man. You really must have a chat about it with your father and try to warn him of the danger. Not that you have any particular evidence — just the girl's behaviour, the long glances at Edward, and a suggestion that she is being secretive about something of great importance to her.

Although you have taken various jobs here and there, from time to time, you live on your father's allowance, and would find it hard to live without it. You also spend all the money you get. There's nothing in the bank.

Structured improvisations offer excellent opportunities to groups of actors or students, all of whom should be invited to devise their own. They are in many ways an ideal bridge towards the devising of full-scale improvised productions, and indeed to one's first ventures in playwriting.

5 Improvised Stages

Whenever the stage we are using is inadequate for our purposes, we seek to improve on it, to render it more flexible — we improvise. Similarly, when we have no stage at all we use the means at our disposal to create one — again we improvise.

The adaptation of conventional stages to render them viable for unconventional productions is increasingly common. The National Theatre production of *The Bacchae* utilised a ramp going down the length of the ground floor of the auditorium and right on to the stage. The production of *Gypsy* took place mostly on a conventional proscenium stage, with the orchestra in the pit dividing the stage from the audience. But in the final section of the show, when the young Gypsy becomes a stripper, a forestage is projected out towards the audience and over the orchestra, and it is here that Gypsy does her burlesque sequences.

In another play at the National Theatre, John Dexter's production of *Equus*, the proscenium stage was transformed by putting part of the audience on the stage itself and behind the acting area, so that the audience, wherever they were seated, could always see other members of the audience. Dexter explained that this idea emanated from the public nature of the psychoanalyst's work, which is the heart of the drama:

> 'I was very aware that one needs a different audience configuration for it, that we should all be observed to be observing. Everyone's in a witness box or an operating theatre during the two-hour span of the play. One was just looking for the shape that would indicate that. When the analyst is most exposed, he's not just exposed internally, privately, but totally and publicly to a whole audience. . . . A proscenium wouldn't give the right tension.'[23]

Elsewhere the improvisation may totally alter the whole concept of the stage, or create one where none existed before. When Le Théâtre du Soleil brought their production of *1789* to the Roundhouse in London, the audience stood in and around the large circular auditorium and watched the action of the drama move to and from a sequence of platforms placed round the outside of the circle. At times the action moved right into different parts of the audience simultaneously, so that one had to choose which particular part of the action to move to and watch.

The possibilities for improvisation are infinite. When Victor Garcia directed and Wladimir Cardoso designed a production of *The Balcony* at the Ruth Escabor Theatre in San Paolo, Brazil, in 1969, they demolished the interior of the theatre to turn the whole auditorium into a massive stage, such that it became:

> 'a sculpture inside of which the actors played, flying in the air . . . the insides of the theatre were torn out from ceiling to basement. Eighty tons of iron were used in making the access ramps and the five circular platforms that could hold 250 spectators at a time. . . . All this machinery may seem gratuitous or excessive, but on the contrary it was absolutely essential and conveyed the play's spirit. Genet's spectacular world was present in the numberless mirrored surfaces; in the chrome-plated gynaecologic table: in the transparent flying saucer that went up and down all during the performance. The scenic space changed frequently . . .'[24]

Not all improvised stages are so spectacular. And of course, just as stages can be moved (and adapted) so can audiences; *1789* moved the audience around the auditorium, like visitors to a fairground, but one could also move the audience from room to room for different scenes or, technology permitting, put them on a revolve which turns round to show a series of stages to them. If theatre still has far to go, so has the audience.

1 and 2   Permanent stage with different kinds of apron

1

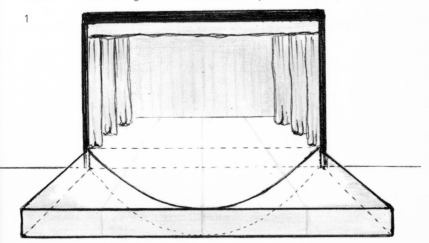

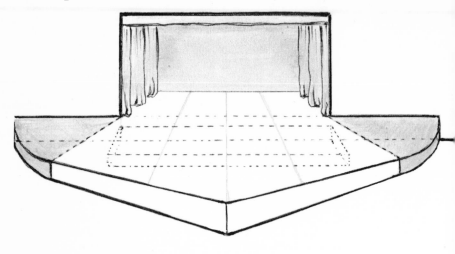

Why improvise?

Apart from the basic situation where we have no stage at all, and hence must improvise or perish (and the artistic dilemma of a stage that is simply wrong for our particular production) a number of technical factors make some form of improvisation essential in many halls and theatres. These will include:

limited acting area on the stage
lack of space backstage or in the wings
bad acoustics
very long hall
low proscenium arch
too few entrances to the stage
insufficient depth to the stage
stage too high from floor level of auditorium
stage floor polished (and so slippery and dangerous).

Such defects are likely to be found in many halls and theatres, and especially in the so-called 'multi-purpose' hall. The latter is almost never suitable for theatre productions, despite the pretensions of its name [25]

The answer to such defects is to get away as far as possible from the stage itself and to think in terms of a more flexible staging, ie either to use the stage in combination with an apron-stage or forestage, or alternatively to leave the stage altogether and employ the techniques of the theatre in the round or 'the theatre in the three quarters'.

We shall look briefly at these three basic possibilities:

1   Apron stages   The first practical step is to see if the stage can be extended by the addition of an apron-stage. An extension of 2 m may perhaps be enough. Or it may be possible to construct a completely independent apron-stage immediately in front of the main stage but at a lower level. This can be of whatever size you wish and of any shape. And it is not necessary to have all the apron at the same level. Of course, where an apron-stage is used with a curtained proscenium stage, you can have scenes in front of the closed curtain, while the setting is changed behind the curtain. See illustrations 1 and 2.

There is an element of impurity in all forms of staging, ie it is virtually impossible to create a stage where all members of the audience see exactly the same thing. All that can differ is the degree of impurity. The conventional proscenium stage offers different views to different parts of the audience, and, of course, in some theatres these views are quite distinctly different. And theatre in the round offers a uniquely different relationship with the stage to each member of the audience. Sometimes the challenge of the particular shape of a stage is met by

3a and b   Independent stages made up of screens standing on or behind a rostra

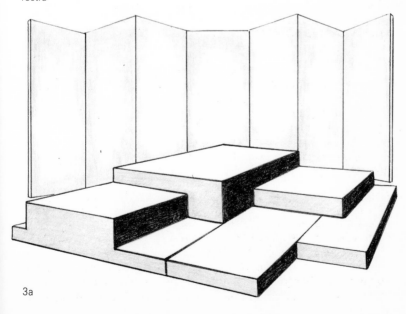

3a

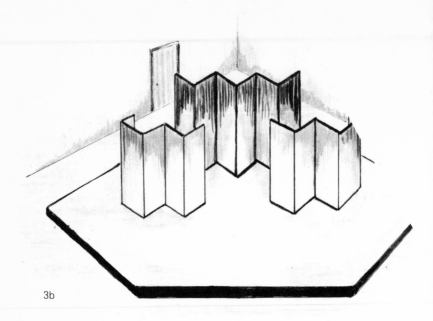

3b

treating it as if it were not there! Thus Irving Wardle recently noted of a production at the Chichester Theatre that it is now the standard practice there to treat 'this defective open stage as if it had a straight edge'.[26] In fact this particular stage thrusts out to the audience with four sides (with the fifth side forming the back of the stage).

Certainly the most basic factor to be considered in any mode of staging is how far we can afford to let different sectors of the audience see widely different things at the same time. At Chichester, for instance, the most expensive seats offer a view straight on to the stage, and across to the back of the stage. It is to these seats that all the productions that I have seen there have been played, and interestingly it is to these seats that the actors have bowed at the end of the play. The less expensive seats offer a view across the stage and to the audience on the other side. So some of the audience see the actors and also other members of the audience, while others of the audience see a more or less stage-filled picture. How far this diversity actually works, and the problems it presents, will need to be worked out afresh with each production.

2 Independent open stages We can also, of course, create stages quite independent of any existing stage, or create a stage

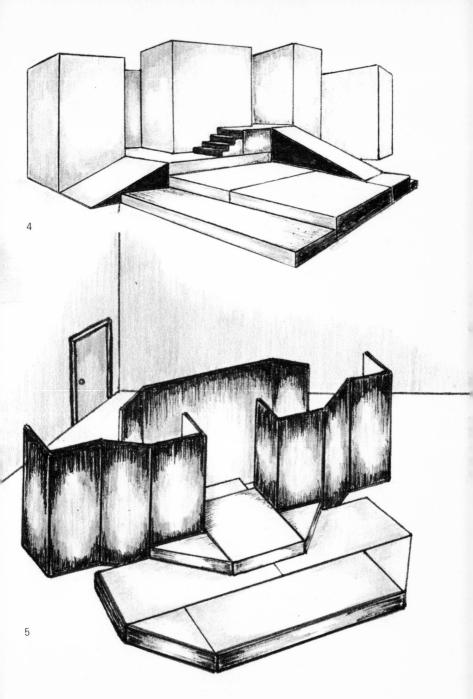

4 and 5   Independent stage made up of flats, rostra, steps and ramps

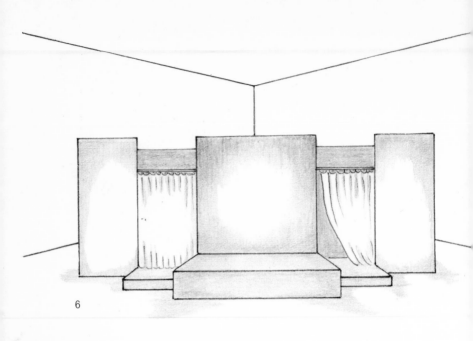

6

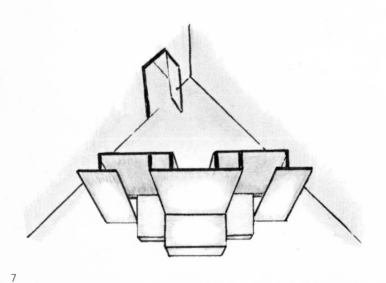

7

6 and 7   Screen-background stage with curtains angled across one corner of
a room or hall. 7 shows a bird's eye view of 6 with backstage and pass door

8

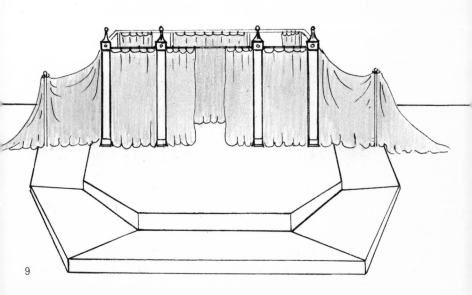

9

8 and 9   Independent stages made up of rostra and curtains

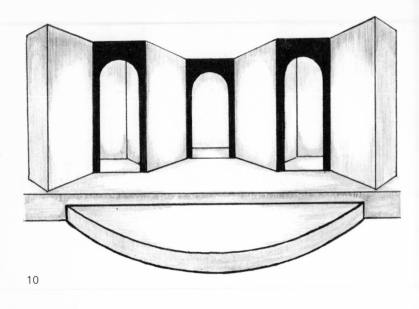

10

11

10 and 11   Formal arrangements of arches for open stage setting

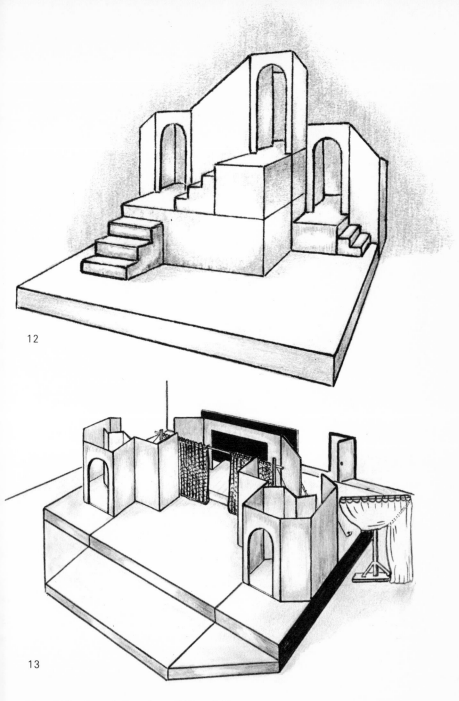

12

13

12 and 13 Extended versions of 10 and 11

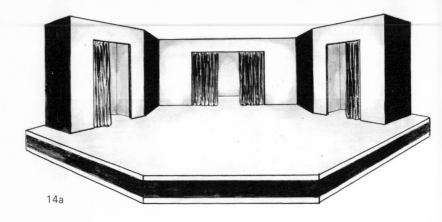

14a

14a Open platform stage with a large arch opening at the back, and two double-door frame arches down right and left

14b The same construction as 14a but adapted for a realistic interior setting on a proscenium stage. The arches are filled in with a door unit and a fireplace unit and at the back with french windows

14b

where none exists. Various facilities can be brought into use for this purpose, whether singly or in combination:

a *Flats or screens* See illustrations 3a and 3b.
b *Rostra, steps and ramps* See illustrations 4 and 5.
c *Curtains* See illustrations 6, 7, 8 and 9.
d *Door flats, arches, etc* See Illustrations 10, 11, 12 and 13.
Illustrations 14 and 15 also indicate how concepts for im-

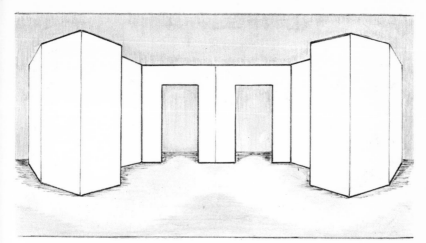

15a

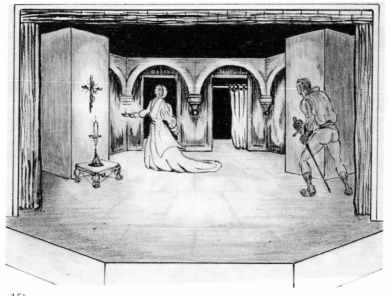

15b

15a   Open platform stage using two door-frame arches
15b   The same construction as 15a but set on a proscenium stage with apron-stage extension
15c (overleaf)   An alternative version of 15a and 15b adapted to the defects of a very small proscenium stage. The setting is built half within the proscenium stage, and half is extended out to an apron-stage built on two levels. The proscenium curtains can be removed altogether or draped up and out of the way

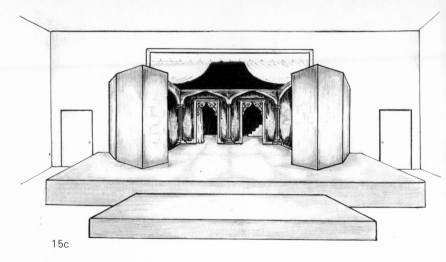

15c

provised stages adapt to (and from) concepts for a conventional proscenium stage design.

Such a list by no means exhausts the possibilities. Scaffolding of any kind is also extremely useful (when it can be acquired cheaply enough) as is all manner of transport, especially for open-air productions, such as lorries, wagons, carts, etc.

3   Theatre in the round   Here the audience completely surround the acting area, which may be round, oval, rectangular or square. Generally speaking theatre in the round should be fairly intimate, with the stage or acting area at ground level. There should be at least two gangways to provide acting entrances, and the audience seating should be elevated in such a way that each row is at least one foot higher than the row in front. Three or four rows are usually enough. Note that since the audience will be looking down on to the floor of the stage, the design and/or the covering of the floor will be important. Furniture will have to be kept to a minimum, and probably nothing taller than an ordinary table should be employed.

Whatever the size of the acting area, the audience must be allowed to see and hear everything that is going on; what is more important they must *feel* that they see and hear, even when various performers are standing with their backs to them. There is no one focal point on such a stage, and no best position.

Costumes assume paramount importance, together with props, in establishing the mood of the production. Lighting will have to be all round the stage, and will need to be set high.

Since theatre in the round involves building up the audience rather than the stage, it is in some ways the most difficult form of staging to improvise cheaply and effectively.[27]

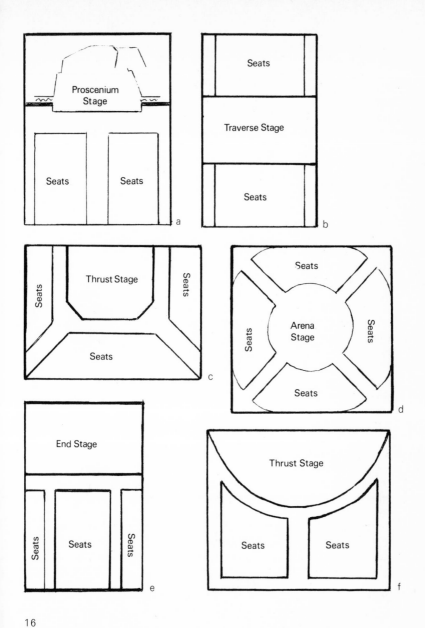

16

16   Simple ground-plans of indoor staging showing the commonest
relationships of acting area and audience.
a proscenium   b traverse   c thrust   d in the round   e end-stage
f alternative thrust

In general: improvised stages

A few general principles may be suggested for working out improvised stages:

1 *Three areas* Any production needs three different areas: the stage on which the actors perform, the auditorium from which the audience view the stage, and the in-between area through which the actors make their exits and entrances. All three have to be thought out carefully, though all three may be endlessly *re*thought. See illustration 16.

2 *Space* This should be the basis of all your thinking; space on stage, backstage, in the audience, in the wings, for the stage management, for the lighting men, etc.

3 *Sight-lines* However you use or improvise the stage, check carefully how far the entire audience can see the action that you put on to the stage. Where the auditorium is lower than the stage, it may be impossible for the audience to see the actors when they sit down, for instance, let alone lie down. This may apply too to apron-stages. All such factors must be carefully watched. Where you improvise your own seating arrangements, this too will have to be worked out from the start of the production.

If you can meet these three criteria, ie you have a space somewhere and it is possible to bring both actors and audience into that space, in such a way that there is room for the actors to act and for the audience fully to see the action, then in one way or another you can create theatre. A stage can be improvised and productions mounted. To give a modest illustration of this: I worked for some time at a college where the only possible theatre space was a long room which had only one door, and of course no stage. We used rostra of various kinds to create a stage, placing it at various levels along one side of the room, with the audience sitting facing it along the other side. We installed lighting and hung it from a pipe running along the top of the wall behind the audience. Since there was only one door it would have created endless disruption to have actors going in and out during a production, and since the room was small it would have been absurd to try to create 'wings'. So we simply had the actors sit down at either end of the room when they came off the stage. The audience accepted this convention, and we were able to make our own theatre with the rather luxurious intimacy of an audience of about fifty and a stage-area that was as large as the seating-area.

6 Stage Design

The concepts for the particular designs for a production will emerge from the shared ideas of the director and the designer, usually working in close collaboration right from the beginning with the costume and lighting designers.

Basic types of design

We can think of stage design as consisting of a number of basic types, which can be used in any number of combinations:

1 The bare stage An effective setting, in fact, and one which concentrates all the attention upon the actors, the lighting and the costumes.

2 Curtain sets Consisting of a bare stage dressed with curtains suspended in the wings and across the back of the stage. See illustration 17. The curtains should generally be dark, and never oatmeal or pink, as these tend to make the actors' faces merge into the background.
  A minor variation of the same idea is to use flats instead of curtains.

3 Painted backcloth and cut-out wings This is the same as the previous type of design, except that a painted backcloth is hung at the back of the stage instead of a plain curtain. Also, instead of the plain flats or curtains hanging in the wings, simple cut-out flats are used to represent some form of actual scenery. See illustration 18. This kind of design is nowadays most closely associated with pantomime and operetta.

4 Simple designs with flats Illustrations 19a–d show simple variations on the basic idea of a set made up with flats, and illustration 19e shows the ground-plan for all four.
  This same idea can, of course, be extended as illustrations 20a and 20b indicate. These show a possible design for a Restoration

17

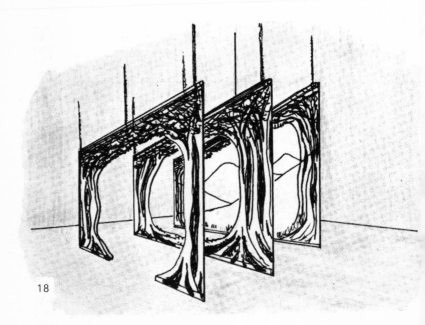

18

17   Curtain set
18   Painted back-cloth with cut-out wings
19a to d (opposite and overleaf)   Designs with flats and arches

19a

19b

19c

19d

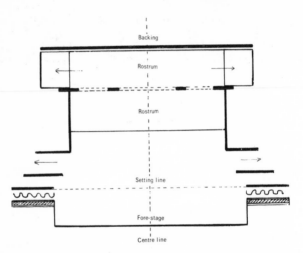

19e

19e   Ground plan for 19a to d

Comedy, and require a stage that is at least 6 m wide and 4·25 m deep. Molière or Sheridan could also be performed against such a setting. The main features of the design are:

 proscenium doors, right and left, opening on to the apron-stage

 large apron

 false proscenium

 small inner stage, curtained to allow scene changes to be made while the action continues on the main stage and the apron

 the proscenium, door piece and the false proscenium can be three separate units all cleated together

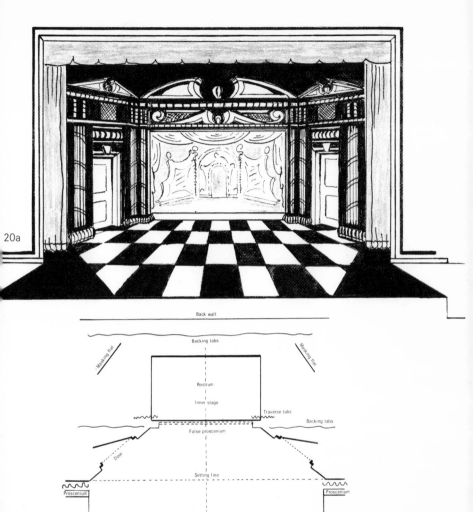

20a   Basic idea for designing a Restoration Comedy
20b   Ground-plan for 20a

the inner stage can be raised, but does not have to be; the
maskings and backings can be curtains, black or any
dark colour
the painted floor is optional
the proscenium doors can open on stage or offstage,
whichever is better
all the decoration, and any perspective can be painted;
on the other hand, moulding and pilasters can be three-
dimensional if the designer so wishes.

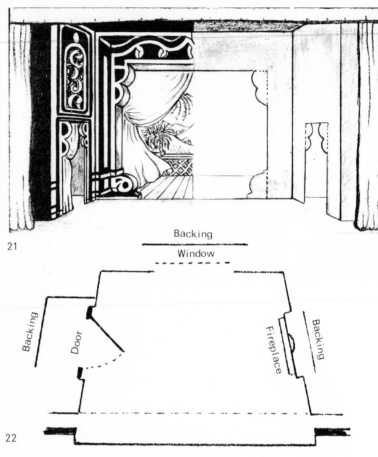

21

Backing

Window

Backing

Door

Fireplace

Backing

22

21 Adaptation of 20a for a Victorian Music Hall
22 Ground-plan for a simple box-set
23–25 (opposite) Variations of a basic box-set to create visual variety and
to avoid unbroken lines of flats.

Illustration 21 shows how the same idea can be adapted to provide a setting for a Victorian music hall or Victorian melodrama. Indeed the Victorian stage was a development from the Restoration stage, with the apron shrunk to a forestage, and the proscenium brought forward.

Instead of doors, this design has two arch flat-pieces set upstage and downstage, with an inner stage above a false proscenium.

5 *Simple box-set* The ground-plan of a simple box-set is shown in illustration 22. The walls are slightly perspected to give an illusion of greater depth. Usually one avoids straight

23

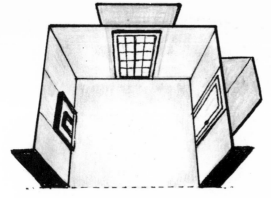

24

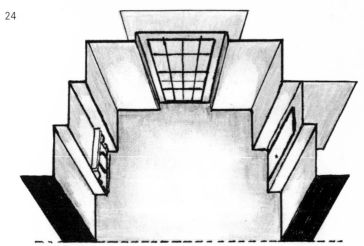

25

26

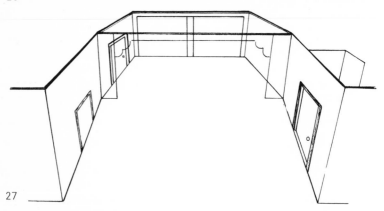

27

26 Box-setting for *Gaslight*
27 Showing the basic simplicity of 26

walls on a stage as they tend to create visual and dramatic monotony. Therefore the walls in this illustration are broken up by the door, windows and fireplace. But where space permits, the best way to break up long straight walls is by angling and recessing, as the next illustrations show.

One basic idea for a box-set can easily be adapted to different stages. See illustrations 23, 24 and 25.

Illustrations 26 and 27 show a box-setting for Patrick Hamilton's play *Gaslight*. This has been chosen to illustrate what is basically a simple and easy conception, as the bird's-eye-view in 27 shows. It also illustrates the way this simple idea can be 'dressed' with furnishings and fittings. This same idea could be adapted into a variety of different atmospheres: Shaw's *Candida*, for instance, or Wilde's *The Importance of Being Earnest*. It could also be fashioned into a setting for an Ibsen play or a Chekov. It may well be that the substitution of, say, a stove for a fireplace becomes the central feature round which the new design is moulded.

Note that the aim of this kind of setting is to re-create an interior with as much reality as possible, so that the audience, while looking at what seems to be a three-dimensional photograph, are drawn into and involved in the drama.

This set can be adapted quite easily for differently sized stages.

If the design involves the use of a ceiling-piece, this will have to be hung first and then kept out of the way while the walls of the set are put in position. The edge of a ceiling nearest the audience is hardly ever flush with the downstage edge of the setting-line; it is usually set at least 1·25 m upstage. Any kind of central hanging lamp or chandelier is usually suspended from a rope of its own and hung immediately in front of the downstage edge of the ceiling-piece.

6 Cyclorama   This can be used on its own to suggest space and distance, but it can also be used in combination with other scenic devices, including pieces of cut-out flats or draped curtains. See illustrations 28 to 30.

Illustration 31 shows the use of black curtains in place of the cyclorama.

Illustrations 32, 33 and 34 show basic ideas for a projected design for *King Lear*, in a surround of black curtains and with a cyclorama behind the curtains. Here the angled, scaffold-like structure is permanent throughout the action of the play; when the black curtains are opened to reveal the cyclorama, a clear scenic contrast is achieved.

A cyclorama, to be fully effective, must be well lit. This will involve floodlighting from above, and two or three troughs or battens lying along the floor with their light directed upwards at the cyclorama. These battens should be concealed behind a black ground-row, about 45 cm high, running the entire width of the cyclorama. This top and bottom floodlighting should give a good overall spread of light to the cyclorama, and if it is circuited up for three different colour changes a good variation of mood can be achieved. Two colour changes will be useful, if three are not possible.

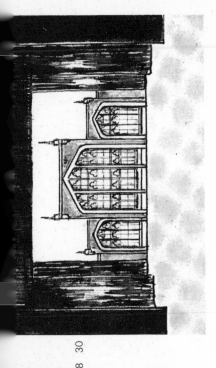

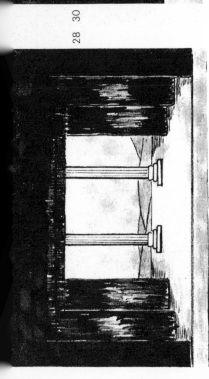

28   Cyclorama with small painted ground row and independent pillars   29   Cyclorama with cut-out flats   30   Cyclorama with draped curtains   31   Black curtains used instead of cyclorama, with decorative screens

28   30

29   31

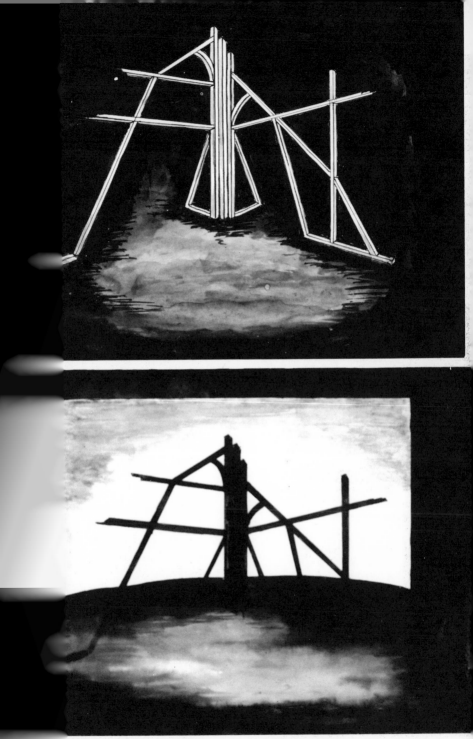

etal set, showing basic ideas for a design project for *King Lear*
in 32, with black curtains pulled back to reveal ground row and
a

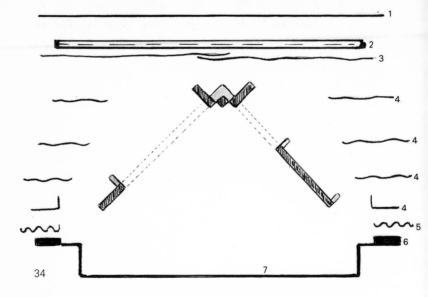

34 Ground-plan for 32 and 33 with markings: 1 cyclorama 2 ground row with lighting batten on floor 3 black traverse curtain 4 black curtains or flats to mask the wings 5 front of house curtains 6 proscenium 7 forestage

Note that to light a cyclorama effectively there must be reasonable depth to the stage. Otherwise the lights directed at the downstage and centrestage areas will spill over on to the cyclorama, and the actors' shadows also will be thrown on to the cyclorama. Ideally, the ground-row battens should be at least 1 m in front of the cyclorama.

If the stage is rather small, then this is an additional argument for building some kind of apron in front of it, perhaps at a different level or group of levels. It is virtually impossible to achieve really interesting atmosphere on a stage which in any way suggests a lack of space, unless of course that is precisely what you are out to suggest.

Note too that with such a setting, black surrounds, ie borders, are essential in order that stark contrasts can be achieved, and so that a great deal can be lost into the darkness.

7   Three-dimensional units built on trucks   These are highly adaptable and useful forms of scenery. It is possible to conceive an entire design in terms of one revolving unit which as it revolves shows, say, three quite different settings. Alternatively a pair of revolves may be devised, which then can be manipulated both separately and together. Note that these units have to be bolted to the floor, if they are to be stable, and that they have to be bolted in two different places, so that one bolt can be undone to swing the revolve round to a new position while being pivoted by the other bolt.

Alternatively double-sided cut-out flats can be built on trucks and moved around the stage in the same way.

Usually, the cyclorama provides an ideal background for such units.

8 *Rostra and steps* All the various modes of staging suggested in Chapter 3 for improvised stages are, of course, also 'designs' and especially right for epics and extravaganzas.

9 *Rostra, steps and scaffolding* Combinations of two or three of these can create extremely flexible and exciting sets. Illustrations 35 to 39 give a variety of examples.

Plan into action

After his initial discussions with the director, the designer will start getting his ideas on to paper in the form of sketches and rough ground-plans. From the very beginning the designer must keep in mind the exact limitations of the stage and the audi-

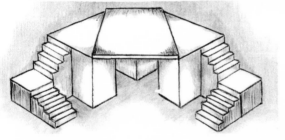

35

35–39 (overleaf)   Varied designs involving the use of rostra, steps and scaffolding

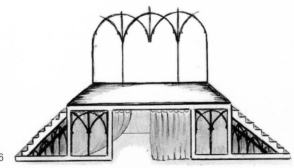

36

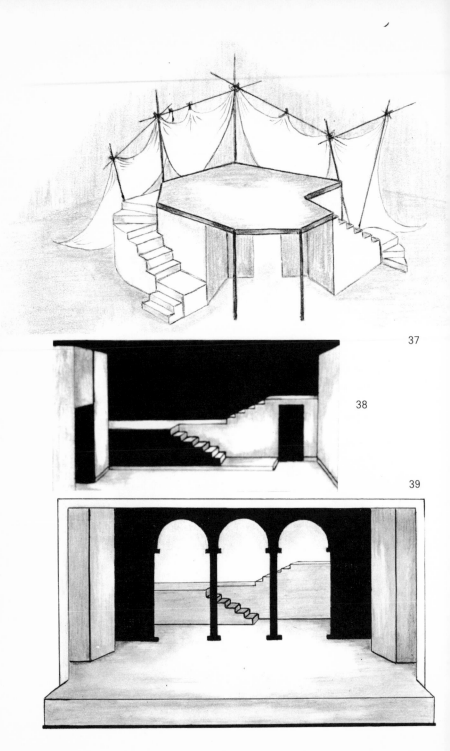

37

38

39

torium. The designer may well produce several different basic ideas, all of which should be thought through very carefully, and all those should be rejected which do not fit sensibly into the limitations of the particular stage. It is remarkable how often designers in the professional theatre as well as in the amateur theatre produce designs which simply cannot be made to work on the particular stage where the production is being mounted; which cannot actually be brought on to the stage at all, for instance, because they are too large, or which involve such lengthy intervals for changing the set that the audience would prefer to go home.

Once the designer and director have agreed upon the basic idea for the sets, the designer then prepares detailed plans. A *ground-plan* is drawn up, usually on a scale of 12 mm to 30 cm. Obviously the designer must first have a ground-plan of the stage itself. See illustration 40.

He will then do an *elevation*. This consists of drawings, on the same scale as the ground-plan, of the various flats or units employed in the designs, numbered to correspond with their numbers on the ground-plan. See illustration 41.

He can also do a bird's-eye-view perspective of the designs, based exactly on the ground-plans. This can be useful to the director and to the actors and stage managers, for it shows clearly how the set will actually work, and how it fits technically into the ground-plan. It is also, for the designer, a good visual preliminary to the making of the scale model. See illustration 42.

Before making the model there should be a conference with all the interested parties, including the carpenters, where all technical points are thrashed out.

It is from the model, together with the ground-plans and elevations, that the sets will ultimately be made.

The *model* will be on the same scale, 12 mm to 30 cm. This is made from an elevation drawn out on thin show card, as in illustration 41. On the elevation, all the flats are laid out side by side in one long straight line, starting with the downstage right flat, nearest to the proscenium arch, which is numbered 1. To each flat is added a flap of extra card to support it when the model is actually stood up. While in this elevation stage, the set is painted in the colours intended for use on the actual stage. Then the designs are cut out and the flap bent so that the model can be stood up. It is useful to have a copy of the ground-plan pinned or glued to a firm base, and to place the model on to this, with the ground-plan numbered in the same way as the elevation.

The next step is to make small, independent scale models of

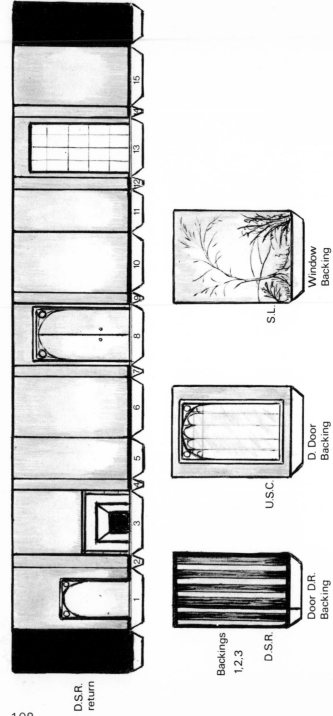

D.S.R.
return

Backings
1,2,3   D.S.R.

Door D.R.
Backing

U.S.C.

D. Door
Backing

S.L.

Window
Backing

40

40   Elevation of 41

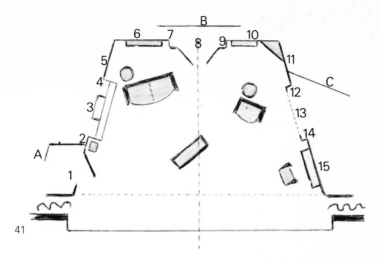

41 Ground-plan (marked with numbers to correspond with 40)

any additional units, such as pillars, fireplaces and staircases. All backings to doorways or windows, and any get-off steps or rostra must also be incorporated into the model.

Finally, the model will need to be fronted by a simple proscenium arch which again is a scaled replica of the proscenium arch of the theatre; assuming, of course, that the designs are actually for use on a proscenium stage.

42 Bird's eye view elevation of 40 with furnishings

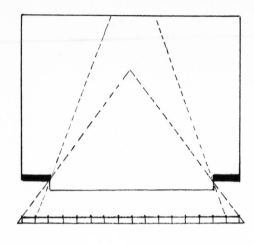

43 Ground-plan of stage and front row of stalls showing sight lines in width, and showing how the narrowing of rows extends the audience's maximum area of vision
44 Sight-lines in height

Sight lines

Central to the whole concept of a design is the question of sight lines. The designer must work out the maximum and the minimum areas of the stage which any member of the audience will be able to see.

This will involve:

1 Masking the sides of the stage with wing flats or curtains so that no part of the audience can see the backstage, and similarly masking the area above the stage with borders. This will not be necessary, of course, if the whole idea of the production and the design is that the audience should see the mechanisms of the stage in full.

The working out of the sight lines is entirely dependent on

the arrangement of seating. Generally speaking, the maximum area of the left-hand side of the stage that is visible to the audience is that part of the stage that is visible to a person seated at the end of the front row of the stalls on the right-hand side. And the wing curtains or flats must be so arranged as to obscure completely his line of vision into the backstage. Similarly the maximum area above the stage that is visible to any part of the audience is that area that is visible to a person seated in the middle of the front row of the stalls, and the borders must be so placed as to ensure that such a person cannot see what the designer does not want him to see. See illustrations 43 and 44.

2   Ensuring that no absolutely vital piece of scenery is invisible to part of the audience. It is not often possible, though, for an entire audience to see *all* the stage, but it is essential that the entire audience see all the actual acting area of the stage all of the time.

Post script

A few final thoughts:

1   A stage can be well designed with quite a modest allocation of scenic devices, especially if the stage itself is regarded as a basis for improvisation. (It must also, of course, be fascinating to have access to all the technology of large professional theatres.) Whatever your facilities, rich or poor, the simpler the design the better.

2   A good design will be right *technically* for the size of the stage (including backstage) and auditorium, and also right *artistically* for the space, shape and mood of the production.

3   A good design will be good to act on, ie easy to move on, not creating technical problems for the actor at the very point where he should be able to put his concentration into his performance.

7 Stage Lighting

General principles

1   Your prime function is to light the actors, not the scenery or the floor of the stage.

2   Time must be allowed for rethinking. No matter how well you work out your lighting in advance, you will probably find there has to be quite an amount of readjustment when the scenery and the lights have been set up.

3   Lighting is greatly affected by the colour of the set. For instance, if the overall colour is a pale one it will create the effect, when the lights are on it, of a very hot stage, and the glare may well bounce back on to the audience. This in turn will reduce the definition of the actors' faces and they will merge into the background. On the other hand a dark set will never look brilliant no matter how much light you concentrate upon it. But the actors will look very vivid indeed, because they will be sharply defined by the darkness of the background.

4   Stage floor-covering should not be at all shiny.

5   In lighting an open stage you will have to rely on front-of-house lights exclusively, and it may well be difficult to decide where to stand them or to hang them. Generally it is no use simply to place them on stands on the floor, for even when extended to their maximum height they are likely to be not high enough. If actors are playing on a raised platform of say, 0·5 m in height, then your lowest standing spot should ideally be 4·25 m from the ground, though you may be able to get away with 3·75 m for some, though not all, of the spots. For reasons such as this, it is essential that the lighting designer is consulted fully from the earliest stages of the production.

6   Any scenery painted dead white and lit without colour filters will automatically be the brightest thing on the stage. This may well be exactly what you want, but be careful!

7   In general, the centre and upstage areas of the stage are illuminated by lights hanging above, or standing on, the stage. The downstage and forestage or apron-stage are illuminated by lights suspended from the front-of-house. See illustration 45.

8   The most satisfactory way to light actors is by *directional lighting*: this involves the use of a fair number of spotlights

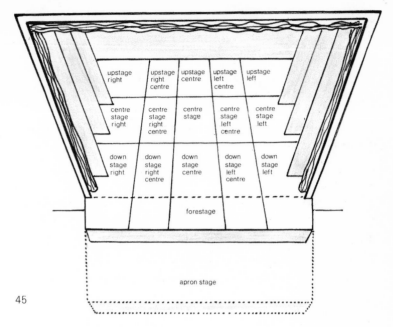

upstage right	upstage right centre	upstage centre	upstage left centre	upstage left
centre stage right	centre stage right centre	centre stage	centre stage left centre	centre stage left
down stage right	down stage right centre	down stage centre	down stage left centre	down stage left

forestage

apron stage

45

45   Acting areas of the stage

together with the judicious and sparing use of a number of floodlights. To light well a moderately sized stage you will need not less, probably, than about fourteen spots and three or four floods.

9   Lights can either be suspended from bars or wall-brackets, or supported on stands. Sometimes it is also useful to put the stands on boxes to achieve added height for the source of light.

Spotlights and floodlights

There are two basic kinds of stage lighting:

1   Spotlights   These illuminate a well-defined area. The major varieties are:

a   *Profile spots*   These have a hard-edged beam. Different shapes can be placed in the gate between the reflector and the lens, and by this means any shape of spot can be produced, such as circular, semi-circular or oblong.

b   *Fresnel spots*   These produce an adjustable circular spot and therefore can be used to illuminate a small or a large area. The light is most intense at the centre of its beam, and it is soft-edged. It is probably the most subtle form of stage lighting, and the most useful.

46 Single spot directed at centre stage

2 Floodlights These illuminate large areas, but they do not have a directional beam and they therefore give diffuse rather than specific lighting. In general, one uses spotlights to light the actors and floodlights to give an added lift to a scene or to light the backcloth or cyclorama. Floodlights may be either single, or in groups encased in long rectangular boxes and called battens.

There are also various spotlight accessories such as rotating colour wheels and mirror balls, as well as 'special effects' spots to produce images such as snow, flames, clouds moving across a sky, and moving kaleidoscopes.

An approach to stage lighting

Stage lighting can be approached in this simple progression:
1 Illuminating the actors with a single spot directed at the centre stage Illustration 46 shows two actors illuminated in a single spot. This allows them to be seen but gives them little freedom of movement. The light is hung from the Number One Spot Bar. This is the bar which hangs immediately behind the proscenium arch. Lights hung from this bar can only illuminate the actor when he is centre or upstage. If lights hung from this bar are aimed downstage they merely light up the tops of the actors' heads.

114

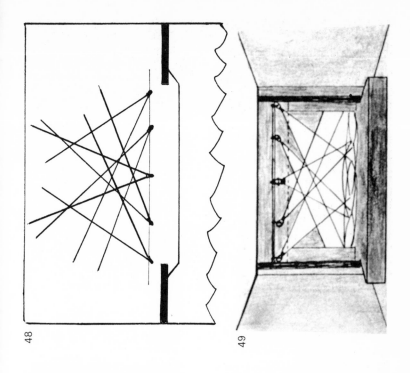

47 Group of spots directed at centre stage
48 and 49 Extended versions of 47

2   Illuminating the actors with a small group of spotlights directed at the centre stage   Illustration 47 shows the addition of two spots, hanging stage left and stage right respectively on the Number One Spot Bar. Notice that the spots are so directed that their light overlaps. This has to be experimented with until an even spread of light is obtained.

Illustrations 48 and 49 suggest a fuller version of the same basic idea: they show a ground-plan and elevation of centre and upstage lighting using five spots hanging from the Number One Spot Bar.

3   Illuminating the actors in the downstage area with spots hanging from the front-of-house   Illustrations 50 and 51 show the illumination of the downstage area by the use of two pairs of spots suspended from either side of the front-of-house. If you add to this the lights suspended from the Number One Spot Bar in the previous illustrations, you will have the principal acting area tentatively covered. Obviously the wider and deeper your stage, the more spot lights will be needed to cover it.

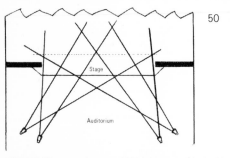

50

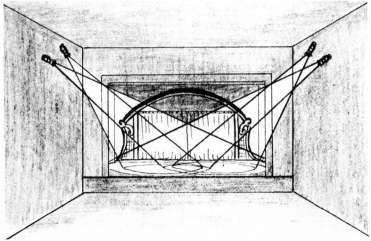

51

50   Lighting the downstage from front-of-house spots
51   Elevation of 50

4 Lighting the actors on the apron   Much the same principle will apply as with the downstage area. Use a couple of spots at each side of the front-of-house, and another couple from the centre. See illustrations 52a and 52b.

5 Lighting the actors in the upstage area   Two further spots can be added to the Number One Spot Bar, hanging respectively one-third and two-thirds of the way across, and with their beams crossing and aimed at the upstage area. On a larger stage you would use the Number Two Spot Bar, which hangs farther upstage.

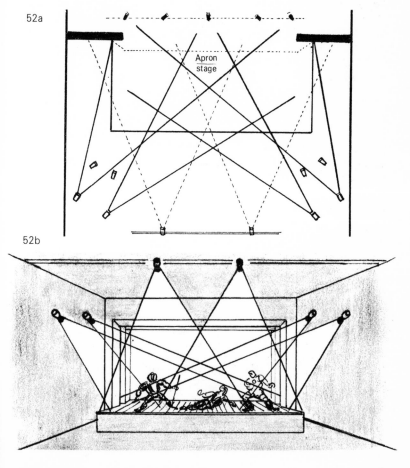

52a   Ground-plan for lighting the apron
52b   Elevation of 52a

6 *Lighting the cyclorama* If you are using the cyclorama to create an illusion of sky, the best way to do this is by hanging a set of batten-lighting from the top of the stage at least 1 m from the cyclorama, using two or three lengths of 2 m each. Also place the same amount along the floor in front of the cyclorama and at the same distance. When you use battens in this way, you should use wide-angled reflectors in each compartment, and if your battens are so circuited that three or four different colours can be used separately, then use one circuit of open white, one of steel blue and one of deep blue, and then mix them until you get the colour you want.

7 *Lighting the backings* These are views seen through, say, doors or windows, and may consist of a painted backcloth, a painted flat, or a portion of the cyclorama. These need to be lit independently of the rest of the stage, and usually by flood-lighting, whether by single floods or battens.

8 *Use of colour filters* In the form of gelatine or plastic sheets these can be fitted in front of spots or floods. These have standard names and numbers, and there are nearly seventy of them, but the most useful are:

Number 3	Straw
Number 17	Steel blue
Number 18	Light blue
Number 50	Pale yellow
Number 52	Pale gold
Number 53	Pale salmon
Number 54	Pale rose
Frost filter	

Various points may be worth noting with regard to the use of colour filters:
a   The deeper the colour, the less light you get.
b   Open white is the maximum brightness possible.
c   Frost filters are useful if the edges of the spot's focus are too hard for your purposes, as it helps to soften them. If you do not wish to lose the power of the light, then a hole can be cut into the centre of the gelatine.
d   The frost filter can be used in combination with any other filters; the frost filter itself is neutral, like frosted glass.
e   A mixture of 50, 52, 53 and 54 will usually give the right kind of balance to the acting area.
f   In general, avoid the deep or the hot colours such as purple, orange or red; use 17 (steel blue) for hard brightness of moon-light.

Lighting the sections of the acting area

1   This elementary approach to stage lighting outlined above is, of course, a simplification, especially with large stages where the acting area may itself be too extensive to split up into conventional divisions. But the same basic principle will apply: think of your entire acting area in terms of sections and then proceed to light each section, using as a general guide the policy of employing two spots to light each section, with each spot aimed from a more or less opposite direction and thus creating a degree of overspill. See illustrations 53, 54, 55a and 55b. The conventional terms for describing the basic areas of the stage are given in illustration 45.

53

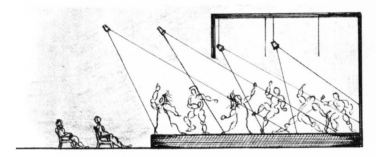

54

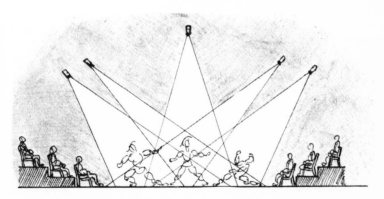

53   Showing in profile the need for lights to overlap in order to obtain an even spread of light
54   Showing need for overall spread of light on an arena stage while being careful not to light the audience

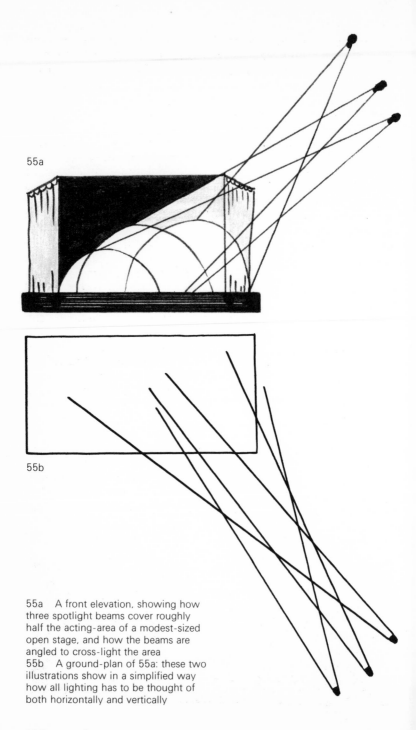

55a

55b

55a   A front elevation, showing how
three spotlight beams cover roughly
half the acting-area of a modest-sized
open stage, and how the beams are
angled to cross-light the area
55b   A ground-plan of 55a: these two
illustrations show in a simplified way
how all lighting has to be thought of
both horizontally and vertically

2 In improvised theatres the front-of-house lights will present a problem, for there may well be no permanent fixture on which to put them. There is also the problem of being able to place them high enough. See illustration 56. If it is possible to fix a grid or bracket either to the side walls or to some other convenient structure, then the lights can be hung from this. A balcony going round the hall can be useful for this purpose, and even if it is not possible to fix brackets to the balcony itself, at least the lights can be put on stands on the balcony.

3 It is important to note that where a light is hung from the *centre* of the hall/theatre, then lack of height is more damaging than in the case of light coming from the sides.

4 In setting up the lights, each flood and each spot has to be set separately. And the lighting director will need at least three assistants: one to position the light, while the second operates the switchboard and the third moves into the various pools of light. The director can then see whether the lights are in the right position and at the right angle. Colour filters are placed inside the lights once they are properly positioned. Each light is set individually against a background of complete darkness, and then in conjunction with the other lights. The process is bound to be a lengthy one. And it may be worth reminding oneself before starting: it is the actors that you are lighting, and especially the actors' faces — *not* the floor of the stage.

5 In devising a lighting plot, remember that in lighting, as in everything else on stage, contrast is essential. Vary your lighting at every plausible opportunity, and do *not* start the play with all the lights you have, unless this is essential. Remember too that you can contrast different intensities of light, as well as contrasting total blackout and light. Epics and extravaganzas probably lend themselves most to experiment with the many possibilities of stage lighting. With revues and music hall, a moving spot can be most useful, manually directed in the course

56 Part of the lighting set up on rostra   56

of the show to follow specific performers.

6   The lighting plot will also affect and be affected by the costumes the actor is wearing. In particular, the effectiveness of costumes on a stage can be ruined by the use of the wrong colour filters in the stage lighting. As an obvious example, if you flood the stage with blue light, then you will tend to wash out the colour of say, pink, orange or red costumes. Just as obviously, blue light thrown on a yellow dress will turn the dress green and will bring out the blue-ness of a blue dress. These are indeed obvious points, but very much to be kept in mind when devising a lighting plot, especially if you are seeking to create a very specific visual effect.

8 Building and Painting

Most scenery, however complex it may appear on stage, is in fact made up of small units. What follows is a brief introduction to the making of those units out of which most of the various ideas already discussed can be put together on a stage.

Flats

A *flat* is a fairly light weight unit of scenery, usually rectangular in shape, and made of canvas stretched over a wooden frame. The height and width of a flat can vary depending on the particular requirements and circumstances. In width, a flat may be anything from 200 mm to 1·8 m or more, but usually if a larger width than 1·8 m is required two flats will be used, either hinged or cleated together. See illustration 57.

1   Construction of a flat   The wood used in the construction of a flat is usually white pine, and the standard size is about 75 mm wide × 25 mm thick (3 in. × 1 in.). This 'three by one' will be cut into lengths to become, when assembled, the frame of the flat on which to stretch, nail and glue the canvas. The frame of a flat consists of two vertical lengths of wood known as the *stiles*, and two horizontal lengths of wood known as the *rails*. To give strength a cross-rail is set into the frame, and always in at least one corner an angled cross-piece is set which is there to ensure that the whole frame keeps its shape. The bigger the flat, the more inner cross-rails there will be; and if the flat is wide as well as tall, then at least one inner stile, running vertically between two inner rails, will probably be set in. See illustration 57.

2   Joints used in a frame   Several different kinds of jointing can be used in the construction of a flat frame. Probably the most used is the mortice and tenon joint. The mortice (or mouth) is in the rail, and the tenon (or tongue) is in the stile. With the inner cross-rail, the situation is reversed, ie the tenon is in the

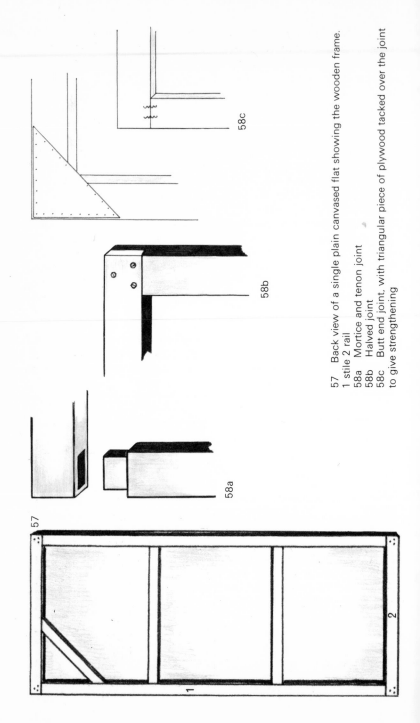

57 Back view of a single plain canvased flat showing the wooden frame.
1 stile 2 rail
58a Mortice and tenon joint
58b Halved joint
58c Butt end joint, with triangular piece of plywood tacked over the joint to give strengthening

rail and the mortice is in the stile. If a flat is to be fairly large, then a mortice and tenon joint is the most serviceable. Smaller flats (not over 2·75 m in height and 1 m in width) can be quite adequately constructed with the use of simpler joints, such as the butt end joint, or the halved joint. See illustrations 58a, b and c.

When assembled, the whole frame is then glued and screwed. Hot glue is used. After gluing the screws are set in each joint. The usual number is at least three screws to each joint. As can be seen in illustration 58b no screws are needed for a butt-end joint. The wooden frame should then be left for twenty-four hours for the glue to set properly.

3   The canvas   The canvas (generally sold in bales either about 90 mm (36 in.) or 180 mm (72 in.) wide) is cut to the required length, and one edge of the canvas, usually one of the two smaller edges, is tacked down on the top or bottom rail of the frame. The canvas does not overlap the sides of the frame, but is so cut that the edge of the frame and the edge of canvas on all four sides are flush with one another. The canvas is usually cut in such a way that it is slightly smaller than the frame by about 5 mm all round. This ensures that it does not wear and tear during use. The tacks are set on the inner edge of the 75-mm face of the stiles and rails, which will leave a loose piece of

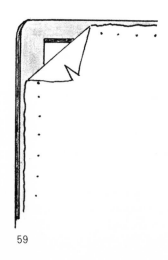

59   Showing how canvas is attached to a frame
60   Two plain canvased flats cleated together

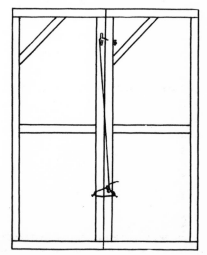

59

60

canvas of approximately 65 mm all round. At each of the four corners of the loose canvas a small piece is cut out, which is usually triangular in shape, and about 37·5 mm long. This helps the corners to lie more evenly when the canvas is eventually glued down. See illustration 59.

During the tacking down of all four sides the canvas is stretched as tightly as possible over the frame. Then the loose piece of canvas all round is lifted and the glue is applied to the wooden frame. The canvas is smoothed down over the glued wood, and any rucks or wrinkling are eliminated with the aid of a rag dipped in hot water.

The flat is then ready for the prime coat of size and whitening. It cannot be painted until it has been primed.

4   Cleating of flats   This is the method of joining two flats together.

On the back and top left-hand side of every flat there is set at about 0·5 m from the top a thin rope. This is the cleat-line.

On the back and top right-hand side of every flat, and set at about 0·5 m from the top is a wooden or metal hook. This is the cleat-hook.

To fix the attached end of the cleat-line, a hole is bored obliquely through the left-hand stile of the flat on the 75-mm surface, which comes through on the inner 25-mm thickness of the stile. The 'line' is threaded through from the 75-mm surface, and a knot is tied in the end of the line and pulled tightly.

The wooden or metal hook is attached to the right-hand stile by means of screws.

To join the two flats together, the cleat-line has to be thrown over the cleat-hook. It is pulled down tightly and hooked round two screws set in the thickness of the two stiles of both flats. These screws are set at about 0·75 m or 1 m from the base of the flats. The line, after passing round the two screws, is then looped through its length and pulled as tightly as possible, and is tied off in a slip knot. See illustrations 60 and 61.

5   Book flats   A book flat consists of two plain flats which are hinged together. The hinges are set into the stiles on the canvased side of the two flats, so that when the two flats are closed up, their uncanvased sides (ie the backs of the flats) are outside. The unit is self-supporting (when opened out like a book) but for real security it is useful to brace it firmly.

With a book flat unit there is always a small gap between the two hinged edges of the two flats. To hide this gap and the hinges, a narrow strip of canvas is glued over them from the top of two flats to the bottom. See illustrations 62a and 62b.

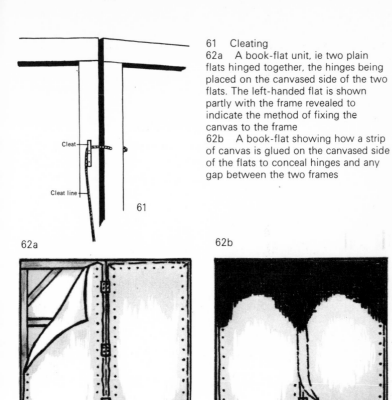

61 Cleating

62a A book-flat unit, ie two plain flats hinged together, the hinges being placed on the canvased side of the two flats. The left-handed flat is shown partly with the frame revealed to indicate the method of fixing the canvas to the frame

62b A book-flat showing how a strip of canvas is glued on the canvased side of the flats to conceal hinges and any gap between the two frames

Cleat

Cleat line

61

62a

62b

A useful variation, is a book flat which is canvased on both sides. This means that both sides of the unit can be painted on and so employed scenically for two separate ideas.

Also useful is the *profiled book flat* and *profiled ground-row* (see illustrations 63 and 64), to which some cut-out piece is attached, usually made with plywood. On the edge of the flat where the profiled plywood will be attached, a 1·25-mm groove is cut on the side where the flat is to be canvased, the depth of the groove being the thickness of the 3-ply cut-out piece. This is glued and tacked firmly into the flat. Then, if the flat is newly constructed, canvas can be stretched, glued and tacked in one piece over both the plywood profile and the frame to which it is attached. It is then ready for priming. If it is an older flat that is already canvased and the profile piece is attached, then a strip of canvas is glued over the join.

6 *Triptych screen and concertina screen* This consists of three flats hinged together, and is a variation on the book flat

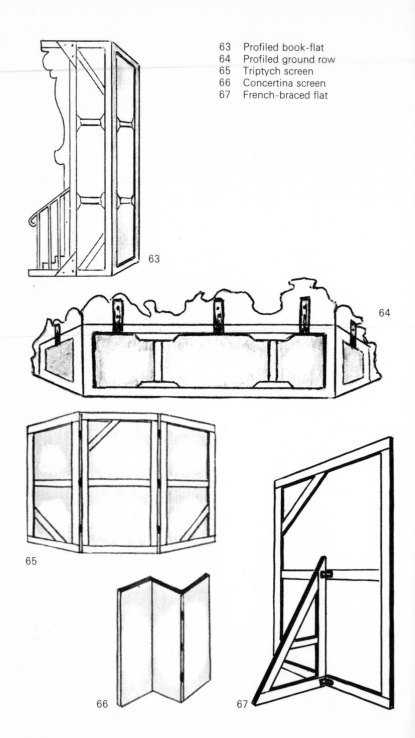

63 Profiled book-flat
64 Profiled ground row
65 Triptych screen
66 Concertina screen
67 French-braced flat

which can be quite workable and useful. See illustrations 65 and 66.

7 *French-braced flat* This is a single plain flat supported by a french brace. A french brace is a triangular wooden frame that is hinged on to the back of the flat, and when it is supporting the flat it is at right angles to it. It is usually held secure by a stage weight. It is especially useful as a unit that can be brought on during the action of the play. See illustration 67 (and also illustrations 68a to 68f which show the different kinds of bracing and weighting).

8 *Door flats* These are made in the same way as plain flats, except that the wooden rail at the base of the frame is cut short to allow an opening into which doors or windows can be fitted. Or they may be used as arches. An iron sill is fixed across the bottom edge of the opening to give strength to the frame, and to help it keep its shape.

There are several different methods of making an arch. One

68 a Sliding wooden brace   b Different base for holding weights
c French brace with brace weight   d Screw as used in (a)   e Weight, as would be used with (b)   f Weight, as in (c)

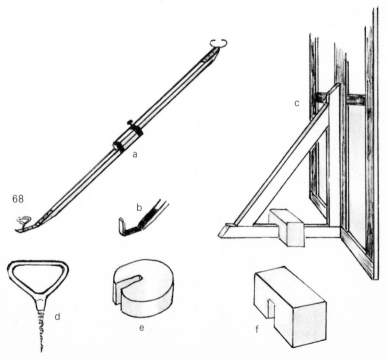

68

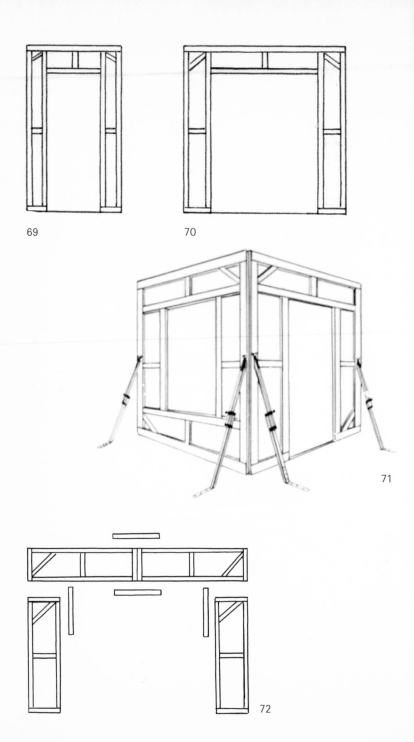

69

70

71

72

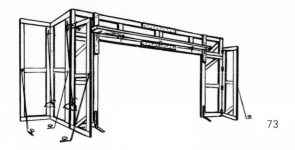

73

69 Door flat
70 Double-door flat (or french window)
71 Back view of door and window flat, cleated together and supported by wooden braces. Doors and window flats that are used by performers always need extra bracing to give reliable strength
72 The basic materials for a small proscenium arch that stands independently (ie not attached to the main permanent structure of a stage/hall)
73 Showing a back-view of the proscenium arch, hinged, battened and cleated, together with supporting wing flats and braces

of the simplest ways is shown in illustration 69. The arch piece consists of a wooden frame, but instead of canvas the arch shape is made from either plywood or hardboard cut to the appropriate size and shape, and is attached to the frame by tacking. As shown in the illustration, the arch piece does not necessarily have a 'reveal', ie a thickness. It can, in fact, be useful with or without thickness, depending on how it is to be employed. See illustrations 69 to 71.

Small proscenium arch

Illustration 72 shows the minimum amount of materials needed for the basic construction of a very small proscenium arch, which might be used with curtains for the framing of an inner stage in a main open-stage setting. See illustration 73.

The arch consists of four flats, all 2·1 m long × 0·6 m wide.

The two horizontal flats are held together by three hinges, and the two vertical flats either side are hinged to the outer side of the two horizontal flats. The vertical flats should also have three hinges for their attachment. Four battens of wood are used to brace the horizontal and the vertical flats together and to keep them rigid.

Illustration 73 also shows two flat frames without canvas, hinged like french braces at right angles, and standing at either end of the main structure. If they are firmly held at the base by stage weights laid across the bottom rail, this should ensure

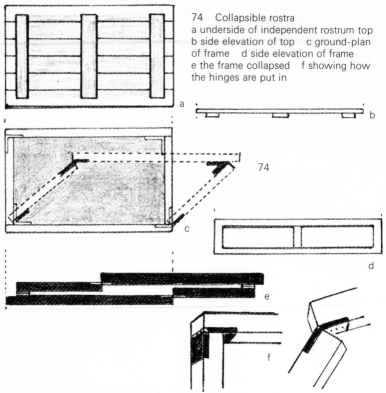

74   Collapsible rostra
a underside of independent rostrum top
b side elevation of top   c ground-plan
of frame   d side elevation of frame
e the frame collapsed   f showing how
the hinges are put in

that the whole structure is well anchored. One or even two iron braces fixed to the offstage sides of the two flat frames will give further security.

'Wing' flats cleated at an angle or right angle to the main proscenium, and themselves supported by adequate bracing, will act as masking flats for the sides and also give further solidity to the whole structure.

Also shown on the illustration is the *shelf* or pelmet board to which the curtain track, pulley rope or wire, and pulley wheels will have to be fixed. The curtains themselves should be as light as possible.

Rostra

The most useful size of rostra is 1·8 m × 0·9 m × 0·6/0·45 m. With only four of these a small stage can be created. The sides of rostra can be frames covered in 3-ply. The top can be made of planking 0·3 m × 1·8 m or 20 mm 5-ply board covering the entire area. The larger the surface the more support will be

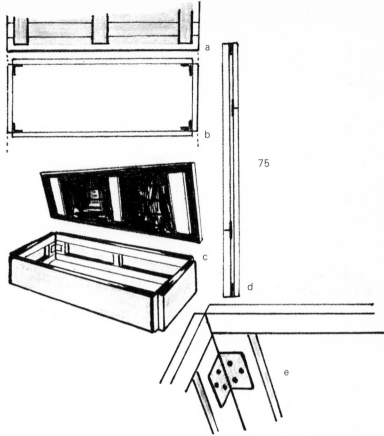

75 Another kind of collapsible rostrum   a rostrum top   b ground-plan of side of the frame   c sketch of (a) and (b)   d collapsed frame of rostra e showing the hinges (compare with 74 f)

needed, with some support at roughly 0·75 m intervals.

Collapsible rostra are especially useful for purposes of trans-portation. See illustrations 74 and 75.

All rostra and steps should be covered with felt, over which canvas is stretched and nailed down and painted with a mixture of scene paint and size. If this is not done, they will reverberate as the actors move across them.

Profile scenery

This is scenery to which a piece is attached in the form of some kind of cut-out. See illustrations 76 and 77.

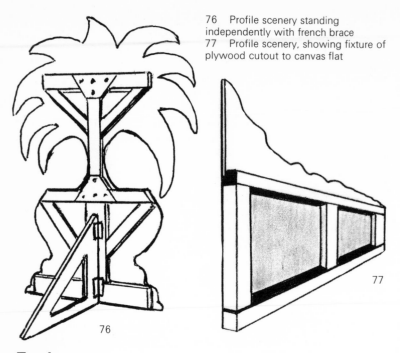

76 Profile scenery standing independently with french brace
77 Profile scenery, showing fixture of plywood cutout to canvas flat

Trucks

These are usually constructed on low movable rostra mounted on castors. The castors are hidden by the surrounding lip or sides of the rostrum. The most practical kind of castor is the swivel castor, which allows the unit to move in any direction. Use silent castors, ie rubber ones, even though they are more expensive. A truck which is say, 1·8 m long, should have six castors: a pair at each end and a pair in the middle.

Fixed direction castors are useful where a unit is moved in front of the audience.

The sides of trucks must not touch the stage. Their whole purpose is to move across the stage without having to be lifted. If the sides are say, 12·5 mm above the floor, then the resulting gap will hardly be noticeable from the front-of-house.

Painting

General principles include:

1 Experiment It is important to experiment with all the various paints or mixtures of paints before actually applying them to the scenery. Try the paints first on some canvas samples.

This is necessary because scene paint creates a lighter colour when it has dried than it does in liquid form in the bucket; this is especially significant where subtle shades of colour are required.

2   Colour filters   Where they are being used in the lighting, it is a good idea to make up odd pieces of canvas painted with the same colours as are being used on the set, and then to throw light on to the canvas through the various filters. Then you can decide exactly how to obtain the effect for which you are aiming.

3   Scene paints   These are usually powdered distempered colours, of which probably the most useful are red, green, blue, yellow, brown, black and whitening. For mixing paints, half-fill an average-sized bucket with the colour and then add sufficient cold water to create a smooth and fairly thick paste. Stir it with a stick until it is all dissolved. No lumps must be left. Then add a solution of prepared size, filling up the bucket. Size is the binder and must always be used.

4   Whitening   Where lighter colours are employed, such as cream or pale blue or pale green, it may be advisable to add whitening to the solution, for this helps to give body or opacity. Experiment beforehand, perhaps on a piece of thick brown paper.

5   Brushes   The essential requirements are:
a   A good laying-in brush (to lay in the basic coat) of 150 mm or 200 mm width, the softer the better to ensure smoothness of surface.
b   Several brushes of different widths, say 100 mm, 72·5 mm and 50 mm. They should be flat like the laying-in brushes, and are for more detailed work.
c   A good selection of lining brushes, from 12·5 mm to 50 mm in width. And do not forget to have a *straight-edge* available for marking long lines, such as stripes on wallpaper designs.

6   Painting the flats   Placing flats on the floor for painting is not a very comfortable technique unless one has long-handled brushes. They can be supported on trestles, or fixed against the wall, with the painters using step-ladders.

New flats must first be primed.

It should be noted that the lining or drawing of details such as panelling or friezes is done *before* the base coat is applied. It is done first in charcoal and then in ink or indelible pencil, the charcoal being blown or dusted off. The lining will then show through the base coat which is painted over it.

Note that in real life colours are not usually simple or unsubtle: a completely white wall, for instance, is never just completely white, for it is affected by age, wear, light and shadow.

7 *Techniques for giving life to canvas* There are various such techniques for making a painted canvas look more interesting. One is the *wet blend* or scumble. This requires a different brush for each colour, and each colour is painted on and blended while they are all still wet, so creating a single colour of greater depth of tone. Another such technique is *sponging* which consists of using a dry sponge or rolled-up rag to dab the basic coat all over the canvas. Or *spattering*, in which you flick the paint on, rather as in action painting.

8 *Textured surfaces* These are surfaces which create any kind of realistic or rough or weathered effect. The most popular form of texturing involves the use of a mixture of whitening and plaster, known as spackel. This is mixed in cold water and then coloured with dye and applied to the surface in thick layers. While it is still damp it can be roughed or grained or 'worked' for greater textural feel. It takes about twenty-four hours to dry. The flat, or any other piece of scenery, should first be painted in the same colour as the dye used in the spackel.

An alternative method is to mix sawdust and/or wood-chips or shavings with the scene paint and to apply the mixture directly as a texturised coat. A little more size is added to the mixture than is usual with straight scene paint and thus the texture coat is bound more firmly.

9 *Stencils* The setting for many plays involves the use of some kind of domestic interior. The best way to set about the painting of such a set is to think about it in two ways: as a reality, and as a theatricality, and then to see how you can amalgamate the two. For instance, although you may want to represent wallpaper on a stage you will not necessarily use actual wallpaper, for it is more costly than scene paint, and difficult to remove if you wish to use the flat again. Also it is often easier to paint a design of the type you want than to find it in a shop. A useful device is the stencil. This can be made either from stout brown paper, or from thin show card. After the stencil design has been cut out (and it is useful to make two or three as a standby) the whole stencil card is painted over with knotting. This is a dark brown liquid and can be purchased from art shops. It makes the stencil waterproof. The stencil should be coated on both sides. If knotting is unobtainable, then quick-drying enamel paint, or gold aluminium paint can be used for the same purpose.

There are two main ways used to apply the scene paint through the design of the stencil. One is to apply it with a brush as drily as possible, dipping only the tips of the bristles into the paint, and drawing off as much surface paint as can be managed. Otherwise the brush will be too full of paint to obtain a clear impression of the design, and the excess paint will run down the canvas after the stencil is removed. The second method is to use a sponge which has first been dipped into the paint and then squeezed out.

If you use a brush, choose a fairly stiff one, not much more than 50 mm in width, and with bristles 40 mm or less in length. If you use a sponge, use one that can be easily held on the hand and not a big bath sponge.

As a complete alternative you may use the method known as *pouncing*: first, the design is pricked out in the stencil-sheet with a sharp pin, the pin-holes being very close together. Then the stencil is placed in position over the canvas while a small cotton bag with powdered charcoal in it is dabbed over the design. When the stencil is removed from the canvas the outline is delicately marked, so enabling the designer to fill in with a brush the different colours as desired. This is, of course, quite a long process.

10 Tapestries To create a stage tapestry use the coarsest hessian or clean rough sacking, and paint it with aniline water dyes. The technique with a largish tapestry is to stretch the hessian on a frame so that the colours sink in easily. Scene paint can be applied to tapestries, but it is best to use it for judicious blending of the outlines. Scene paint will tend to give the tapestry an overall stiffness, whereas you may want it to hang in soft folds. (Do not use dyes on ordinary canvas flats if you wish to use them again, for the dye will always show through any later painting.)

11 Windows If you want to make your windows opaque, then three materials can be used: scenic linen (sometimes called book-linen); linen tracing paper; or ordinary tracing paper (which is very vulnerable, of course, to wear and tear).

If you wish to create stained-glass windows, then stretch the opaque linen across the back of the window frame, making sure that it is tightly and evenly stretched and that it is held securely by gluing and tacking. Then draw the outline of your design lightly in charcoal. If the linen has a shiny surface make sure that it is facing the offstage side of the set. Use aniline water dyes for colour, and if possible work with a light behind the window, so that you can see the effect as you go.

To create an effect of lead, use thick black scene paint.

Where a small stained-glass window is required, for say, a Victorian hall door, you can use pieces of coloured gelatine (stage light filters). It is best to mount these on the back of a design cut out in plywood or thick card.

12 *The spray gun* A useful weapon, especially for spraying on a fine coating of paint to give an effect of age or dirt. But use it sparingly. It is not of any use for painting the base coat, for it creates far too fine a coat.

In general:

a   When painting the basic colours, keep changing the direction of the brush-strokes every three or four strokes. This helps to pull or knit the brush-work together.

b   Do not forget to paint all edges of flats.

c   Always mix plenty of size with each bucket of colour.

d   In marking out any necessary measurements on the flats, such as the layout of panelling, always proceed upwards from the base of the flat, not the reverse.

e   Always be prepared to do quite a bit of final painting and touching up when the scenery is actually set up on the stage. Time must be set aside for this when planning the final stages of rehearsal.

f   The one colour with which to be very careful when painting the set is pink. It is so similar to the colour of flesh that the actors' faces disappear into it.

9 Stage Management and Production Management

I have several times suggested in this book that many an otherwise good production fails in performance because of the poorness of the stage management. Props are not available at the right time in the right place; items of scenery suddenly start to fall over; the curtain closes inexplicably several minutes before the play is over. Everyone who has ever been with any regularity to the amateur theatre can tell the tale of some such calamity. The sad thing is that apparently technical faults of this nature destroy not only the artistic enjoyment of the audience, but the artistic satisfaction of the performers also. The basic principle of good stage management is that every fault is avoidable provided one plans ahead with sufficient care and concern. Such foresight is impossible when, as so often happens in a certain kind of amateur theatre, the stage manager and his team are recruited only days before the production actually goes on the stage. As a college lecturer in drama I quite often receive requests from local amateur groups for a good-natured student who would be interested to stage manage a show that is actually being performed the following week!

Both the stage manager and the production manager, whose work I will discuss separately, must be a part of the production team right from the very start. They must be brought into the initial discussions with the director, the designer, and the lighting director, and any other personnel whose contributions have to be related to each other in some detail if the production is to run smoothly. The actors also will learn much from these discussions if they are given the chance to attend.

Stage management

The stage manager's work will include the following:

1 *At early rehearsals*   He will ensure that the room or hall is well set up for the rehearsal to take place; this may include clearing away a space for the acting area and also marking the floor with chalk or with tape to indicate the limits of the acting

area. In this way the actors rehearse in a space that is the same as the acting area of the stage where they will eventually perform. He will also record all of the director's instructions for the actors' moves in his own copy of the script. (Actors will, of course, do this also for themselves, and it is best done in pencil, so that alterations can be made easily.) The particular system which he employs in order to record all these instructions can be worked out afresh by each stage manager, but it must be a system, and it must be one which enables the stage manager or his assistant to say confidently what he has written down. Simply writing the move into the bound copy of the script is often useless, especially if the script is written on both sides of the paper. In such cases it is best to remove the binding, put the loose sheets into a ring binder, and place blank sheets between all the pages. You can then number each move on the script, and write out the number with the details of the move on the blank sheet that you insert alongside it. It is worth adding that it may be useful to record the moves even where the director does not expect the actors to keep religiously to them at every rehearsal. At least, then, if the actors want to know what they did last time, the stage manager can tell them. Moves are generally given (and recorded) with reference to the acting areas of the stage, and with reference to the furniture and to other characters. So the actor will move say upstage centre — and this will be recorded as UC — or below the sofa (meaning the downstage side of the sofa) or to the left of the King . . . and so on.

It will take time for both the stage manager and the actors also to record the director's instructions, and at those rehearsals where such instructions are being given for the first time (and perhaps for the second and third times also), the director must allow the company time to write down and to check all those things that he wishes them to remember.

2   *At later rehearsals*   He will also be much involved in co-ordinating all the various technical aspects of the production. Generally he will have a team of assistants, each of whom will assume responsibility for a certain aspect of the work involved. This may include someone in charge of props, of furniture, of curtains and also of prompting the actors. Whether or not you finally employ a prompter will depend on the philosophy and experience of the director and of the actors. If you do employ a prompter it is absolutely essential that he should know the production backwards and be fully involved in the rehearsals. The stage manager will also co-ordinate with the lighting director and the electricians to ensure that the lighting plot involves no technical snags and difficulties.

The term plot in this context means the details of the organisation of the particular aspect of the production, so that the lighting plot is the total number of light cues involved and their place in the script. There may also be a property plot (if props are involved) and similarly a furniture plot. Again, no matter what system is employed, the stage manager must ensure that someone is responsible who fully knows his job, and that the details of his job must be written down in some way that is clear and helpful to all concerned.

As the various technical needs of the production become apparent, the stage manager and his assistants provide a substitute for them at rehearsal. So if, for instance, an actor needs a particular prop then he is provided with something to serve in its place until such time as the real thing can be produced. This will apply obviously to furniture also. Likewise, if the changes in lighting are central to the action of the drama it will be helpful if the stage manager calls out the lighting changes at rehearsals, even though it will be a long time before you work in the real theatre with the real lights.

3 *At dress rehearsals and performances*   He is entirely responsible for the running of the show: the co-ordination of all the technical aspects of the production is his concern, from the fading out of the house lights to the final curtain. This does not mean he does any of these things himself. He organises everybody else. And the dress rehearsals are the time when he puts his organisation to the test, and irons out any remaining faults. It is he who is responsible for everything that happens backstage, not the director. Indeed the director who hovers backstage either at dress rehearsal or at performance is a nuisance to everyone else, and especially to the stage manager.

The task, then, of the stage manager is to ensure that everything is technically ready for the performances, and this means that he is also responsible for setting-up the scenery on the stage itself. Whether or not the stage manager also assumes responsibility for getting the actors on to the stage at the appropriate time will depend on the stage manager himself and on the facilities at his command. I think it is fair to say that the system of calling the actors from their dressing rooms to the stage is falling out of use, and that actors are expected to act as their own call-boys.

4 *Sound plot*   There will also need to be an assistant stage manager in charge of all sound cues and effects. As with the props and lighting cues, a complete *plot* of the cues will need

to be drawn up so that the person responsible, and everyone else, can see clearly what is happening. As regards music it is clearly preferable to have the music performed live rather than have it played over on a gramophone, though there may well be very good exceptions to this rule. As regards *sound effects*, the superiority of taped or recorded effects over live effects will depend chiefly on the quality of the equipment that you have available for playing back the effects to the audience. Obviously a single tape recorder or record player will tend to be inadequate, even in quite a small auditorium. If the sounds are to have a three-dimensional quality they need to come from more than one source. So everything will depend on the quality of the amplification and the number of amplifiers at your disposal, and on where the amplifiers can be placed.

Sound effects can be purchased on tape and record from a number of companies. Their addresses can be obtained from *Contacts*, which is published by Spotlight Ltd. Details are given in the reference section at the end of this book.

All music is protected by the laws of copyright. For permission to use recorded music you should apply to Phonographic Performance Ltd, Evelyn House, 62 Oxford Street, London W1. For permission to perform copyright music (ie music by a composer who is either living or has died within the last fifty years) you should apply to the Performing Rights Society, 29 Berners Street, London W1.

Production management

Where the stage manager is in charge of all technical matters, so the production manager is in charge of all administrative matters. Again, he will need a team of people working under him, and between them they will ensure that the business side of the production runs smoothly. This will include:

1 Costing the production, and working out how the cost is to be distributed among the various departments: costumes, scenery, lighting, royalties, etc.
2 Organising the publicity.
3 Organising the printing of programmes and tickets.
4 Organising the sale of tickets.
5 Organising the front-of-house.
6 The payment of bills.

It goes without saying, that the more ambitious the project the greater the tasks of the production manager. Where theatres have to be booked, or tours organised, all such matters fall within his province. Again, it is essential that he is involved in the production right from the start.

Obviously, within the professional theatre and also in the large and well-established amateur companies the tasks I have allocated here to the stage manager and the production manager will often be performed by personnel whose official titles vary greatly from one company to another. But the tasks themselves remain of central importance to the production, and must be thought about alongside all the other non-technical and non-administrative aspects of the production.

Within the professional theatre, too, the various people fulfilling all these roles will be more or less expert in so doing. The stage manager, for instance, is quite likely to be the most truly professional person in the entire production team, and perhaps more accomplished in his field than the artistic director in his field. Outside the profession the situation is often entirely different: the idea for forming a company or for staging a particular production usually generates from the enthusiasm either of the director himself, or the director and some of the actors. Perhaps there is no prospective stage manager, or lighting director, or production manager in these early phases where the idea is first explored. This may well mean that the artistic director has not only to recruit these other personnel but also teach them their jobs. This is certainly true of a large number of amateur productions in which I have myself been involved both within education and elsewhere. The amateur director, to a greater extent than the professional director, needs to possess many theatrical skills if he is to be able to do his job thoroughly, and must be prepared to train many members of his production team.

10 Stage Make-up

1   There are two basic purposes which can be achieved by painting the actor's face: to emphasise clearly the natural features of the face, and to disguise those features. In the latter case we usually speak of it as a character make-up as opposed to a straight make-up. Both of these purposes are directly related to stage lighting. Only very exceptionally would you make up an actor's face if he is performing in a small room, for instance. And similarly, the smaller the theatre the less likely it is that the actor will need make-up. Here, as in all things, the conventions change, and the actors in many of the smaller London and provincial theatres are less likely to employ stage make-up today than even twenty years ago.

2   Fundamentally, stage make-up is necessary where the stage lighting is so powerful that it robs the face of its natural contours and colouring. The aim of the make-up is to restore them. There are, of course, also plays whose style demands not only that the actors should be made-up, but also that they should appear to be made-up to the audience. This is true of some of the characters in Restoration Drama, and in pantomime, for example. But apart from such instances, make-up fails in its intended purpose, and can even ruin the play entirely, if the actors look as if their faces have been painted.

3   Stage make-up can only be adapted to the face of the particular actor who is wearing it; for this reason it is always best for the actor to learn to do his own make-up and to experiment until he achieves good results. All stage make-up has to be adapted to the basic shape, colouring and appearance of the actor's face.

4   Generally, in the use of make-up one distinguishes between *sticks* of make-up, which are applied directly to the face in order to make a base of colouring, and *liners* (smaller and thinner versions of the sticks) which are usually applied to the palm of the hand and then painted on (with a paint brush or a thin stick) to create lines and shading. If a beginner wanted to know which specific items of make-up he should start to collect, I would recommend the following, made by Leichner Ltd:

Sticks   No 5: pale creamy yellow, useful as a foundation to provide the base. Other colours can be added to create various kinds of complexion.

No 6½: muddy grey, useful for mixing with 5 to create age.

No 8: brownish-red tan, useful when mixed with 5 to create a foundation colour of ordinary healthiness, especially for men. Women may find No 4½, which is a pinkish sun-tan, more effective than No 8.

No 9: brick-red, can be mixed with 5, and with 5 and 8, to create various tones of complexion.

Liners   Lake, medium brown, dark brown, black. All of these will be useful for lining and shading.

The beginner will also need, of course, a fine paint brush, powder, powder-puff, removing cream and plenty of tissues.

5   A *straight make-up* for men and women could be along these lines:

Foundation   No 5, with No 8 or 9. Women tend to use 4½ instead of No 8. The grease paint must be spread evenly with the finger-tips over the face and down into the neck. Extra colouring can be added to the cheeks, if necessary, by using No 9. Women sometimes use the Leichner Carmine 11 for this purpose.

Eye-shadow   Women can also use an eye-shadow that tones in with the colour of their eyes, and for especially glamorous or exotic effects they can use silver or gold.

Eye make-up   Dark lines painted close to the edges of the eye-lids help to give prominence to the eyes. The actual colour used will depend on the colour of the actor's hair. Generally, men with black hair use a black liner, those with dark brown hair use a dark brown liner and those with red or fair hair use medium brown. Women, whatever the colour of their hair, can have a much more obviously made-up appearance, and can use black

78

78   Eye-line make-up for men, showing a fairly simple method, which emphasises the shape of the eye without too much exaggeration. The cream paint at the outer edge gives the effect, from a distance, of making the eyes look more widely set apart, and also makes each eye look larger. If a simpler method is required, then paint on only one line — the one shown painted below the lower lid

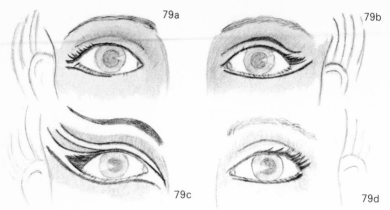

79 Four different eye-line make-ups for women   a a simple straight eye make-up   b a highly stylised eye make-up for immortals and such like. It can be done in a number of different ways — this illustrates only one variation in how to create an exotic eye make-up. Colours are also optional. For example, heavy dark lines can be black, purple, or brown. White, pink or cream can be used for the light parts. Eye-shadow can be any exotic colour desired, such as gold, silver, green, mauve or red, and where necessary, more than one colour can be used at a time   c a more extravagant version of (a)   d shows emphasis of the actual eye shape only, used with false eyelashes, or where mascara has been used heavily

or dark brown, and mascara for eyelashes. The lines are best painted on with a firm paint-brush: draw a clean line from the centre of the upper lid outwards to the outer side of the eye, and a fraction beyond. Do the same on the lower lid and extend the line a little beyond the outer side of the eye. Do not let the two lines converge. For added clarification of the eyes, if necessary, you should then paint a thin line of pale cream (No 5) between the outer edges of the two dark lines. If it is appropriate, you can also paint up the eyebrows in the same colour as you have used for the eye lines. But be careful not to make the eyebrows look unnatural. See illustrations 78 and 79.

Lips   Women may need to use a little of Carmine 11, and men may need a little of No 8 or No 9.

Highlights   Occur naturally where the bone structure of a face is most prominent. They can be accentuated by a careful application of No 5 to give sharper definition. But actors who possess very strong features, such as a prominent nose and cheek-bones, will not need to paint on highlights. See illustrations 80 and 81.

6   When drawing *lines of age or character* on to a face, remember that lines as such will not stand out when the stage lights are on them, unless they are part of an overall contrast of light and shade on the face: it is the contrasting of light and shade which forms the basis of stage make-up. The light part

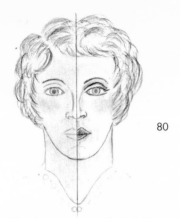

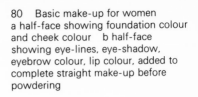

80 Basic make-up for women
a half-face showing foundation colour
and cheek colour   b half-face
showing eye-lines, eye-shadow,
eyebrow colour, lip colour, added to
complete straight make-up before
powdering

80

81

81 A young woman's straight
make-up completed. A little painted
highlighting can be applied to the
bridge of the nose and above the
eyebrows (using No 5 grease paint) in
order to give a little more definition
to the features, should it be required.
This may be necessary if an actress is
working in a large theatre or hall.

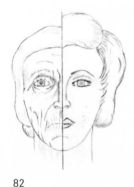

82

83

82 Half-face old-aged character make-up.
83 Half-face preparation for an old-hag type of make-up. A foundation of
No 5, No 6½ and No 8b may be quite effective. Shading and lining can be a
mixture of Lake and No 7. No 5 overlaid with No 20 for highlighting. Create
unnaturally large nostrils with Lake and No 7. Tiny irregular blobs of Carmine II
or III as near as possible to the lower lid will help to give the eyes a blood-shot
look. If there is need for an extra grotesque look, try adding a false hooked
nose

84 Full-face realisation of 83 with the addition of a wig. A special tooth enamel can be obtained for blacking out teeth, if such an effect is desired. For a temporary view of such an effect, wipe the tooth or teeth to be blacked out dry with a paper tissue — paint with black grease paint. If the effect is right then get an enamel for use during a whole performance

84

85 Ground-work for ageing character make-up. The main areas of a face are shaded and highlighted to indicate clearly where shading and highlighting will be needed as a ground-work on which to build an ageing character make-up

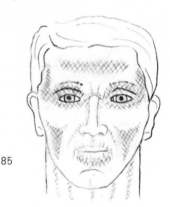

85

a b

86

86 Completed version of 85
a Half-face showing foundation colour and shading completed but without highlighting or lining
b Character make-up with added painted highlighting and lining

148

stands out, and the shaded part almost disappears. But you must have the contrasts for any effect to be made. If you highlight the cheek-bones, for example, and shade in the cheeks themselves, then you create an effectively gaunt appearance. See illustrations 82 to 86.

Lines should be painted on with an orange stick or a paintbrush. It is best to paint on only a short line, about half the length required, so that the line can be finished off by dragging down the line of paint with the little finger of either hand, so that no hard ending is left.

When you paint the make-up on to the face with a stick or brush, you apply the paint first to the palm of the hand which you then use as a palette. With the other hand you then use the brush to paint on the colour to the face.

7   In *preparing the face* to receive make-up hair must be kept well out of the way, with hairpins, scarf, etc, and the face and hands must be washed. Many actors also smear their face with removing cream or skin lotion and then remove the cream with paper tissue: this helps the application of the make-up.

8   Grease-paint generally needs to be *powdered* once the make-up is complete. Using some kind of powder-puff, apply the powder liberally, but do not rub or drag the puff over the paint. The generous application of the powder helps to fix the make-up and stop it from running or smudging during the performance. To remove surplus powder, use either a very soft powder brush or a very fluffy puff. If the face still looks too powdered, gently sprinkle cold water all over it, and then, with soft paper tissues, dab the face dry.

9   *Hands* need to be made-up to correspond with the make-up that is applied to the face. If, for instance, a face is made to look very old, then you might apply highlighting to the bones of the hand with No 5, and then shade in the skin between the bones with a combination of Lake and No 7. The veins could then be delineated with blue liner. All this is done to the back of each hand. The palm of the hand would not need to be made-up.

10   As regards the use of *wigs* on stage, the best advice is to avoid using them unless they are absolutely essential. It is extremely difficult to hire wigs which fit well and look right. If you *must* have a wig then make quite sure that you give the hiring firm your correct measurements. If, despite this, the wig is loose-fitting, then an unobtrusive tuck can be made on the inside of the wig, at the back, with a needle and thread. If the wig is too tight, there is, of course, little that can be done.

Most wigs nowadays have a shaped piece of hair lace or net which protrudes about half an inch beyond the hair-line of the wig, and across the forehead from ear to ear. This can be attached to the forehead by spirit gum. From the audience, the hair lace is pretty well invisible.

11   *Beards and moustaches* can be made up with crêpe hair. This is usually sold tightly plaited around two lengths of string. When it is unravelled it is tightly waved or crimped. To get rid of this waviness, unravel the length you require, and cut off the two loose pieces of string. Take up the hair and steam out the waviness by holding the unravelled length in front of the spout of a boiling kettle.

It should be stressed finally, that make-up is dictated by the quantity and quality of the stage lighting. Even in large theatres it is perfectly possible to dispense altogether with the make-up if the lighting is sufficiently well devised, in the judgment of the director, to preserve the three-dimensional features of the face.

Glossary of Terms Used in Staging and Production

Acting areas   These represent the whole area of the stage that is visible to the audience. They are usually thought of in divisions, as in illustration 45.

Apron-stage   Any kind of addition to the stage, permanent or temporary, and built in front of the proscenium.

Backcloth   A large, high and wide canvas with wooden battens at the top and base.

Backing   A piece of scenery usually made up of a flat or flats, which is seen through an opening such as a door or window, and which conceals anything behind it and offstage.

Batten   A length of wood.

Blacks   A set of black curtains suspended in the wings, across the back of the stage, and across the top of the stage (borders), thus surrounding and enclosing the acting areas of the stage.

Boat truck   A low platform on wheels or castors, on which scenic items can be built and moved.

Book flat   Two flats hinged together, which when opened like a book will be self-supporting.

Borders   Long strips of canvas or cloth hanging one behind the other and stretching from stage left to stage right. Used to conceal from the audience's view anything above the *top* of the scenery. The usual number on an average stage is three.

Box-set   See illustrations 23 to 26.

Brace   A wooden or iron piece for supporting scenery. See illustration 68.

Ceiling-piece   A flat hung by ropes and then lowered into position so that it rests on top of the box-set flats and forms a roof or ceiling. It is always made large enough to extend beyond the edges of the flats, both at sides and back, by about 0·6 m.

Cleat, cleat-line   See illustration 61.

Composite set   A set in which several different localities are incorporated into one design, perhaps with each locality on a different level. Or a single stylised setting where different places are represented chiefly by changes of lighting, but without any one part of the design representing any visibly specific place.

Counter-weight   A round iron weight used to weight down braces. See illustration 68.

Cut-out flat   Also known as a profile flat. See illustration 63.

Cyclorama   See Chapter 6.

Dock   The area backstage, used for storing scenery.

Downstage   The part of the acting area which is nearest to the audience.

Edges   The very important *thickness* of the flat, often forgotten when painting.

Elevation   See illustration 41.

False proscenium   A temporary arch set upstage of the permanent proscenium.

Flat   A unit of scenery made of canvas stretched out on a wooden frame.

Flies   The space above the scenery or setting, where scenery can be hung or 'flown' while not in use.

Floats   See footlights.

Floodlights   See Chapter 7.

Footlights or *floats*   Floodlights placed in the floor immediately in front of the proscenium curtain.

Front-of-house   The auditorium.

Front-of-house spots   The spotlights fixed in the front-of-house. Not to be confused with the house lights.

Front-of-house tabs   Main proscenium curtain.

Gels   Shortened word for 'gelatines' or 'jellies', colour filters placed in front of spotlights.

Ground-plan   Scaled drawing of the set as viewed from above.

Ground-row   A low piece of independent scenery, often placed a few feet downstage of the backcloth or cyclorama and perhaps used to hide any lighting battens used to light the backcloth or cyclorama.

House lights   Lights which light up the auditorium.

Inset   A small setting inside another one, used for example in a prologue and then removed.

Lighting batten   A length of wood or steel rod to which are affixed lights.

Lines   Ropes.

Masking-piece   Anything such as a flat or curtain which is used to conceal anything from the audience. Usually such pieces are 'backings' to doors or windows.

Offstage   Any part of the stage that is not seen by the audience.

OP Side   Short for the side opposite to the prompter's. Traditionally the prompter sits on the side to the actors' left.

Pin-hinge   A hinge whose two pieces are pivoted together by a pin.

Profile flat   See illustration 63.

PS Side   Prompter's side. The actors' left (ie the actors' left when facing the audience).

Props   Any portable items or properties brought on or taken off during the course of the play. Props table — where the smaller props are kept, usually in the wings stage left.

Proscenium   Roman term for the area on which the actors actually performed. Nowadays we use the term chiefly to refer to the proscenium arch, which is the main arch at the front of the stage, separating the stage from the auditorium.

Rails   Horizontal framework of a flat.

Raked stage   A stage sloping upwards from the proscenium arch.

Ramp   A raked rostrum.

Returns   The two black flats which flank both sides of the set, and are placed about 0·6 m from the proscenium arch and run offstage parallel with the proscenium arch. They mark the sides of the downstage edge of the sets.

Reveal   Unit added to the flat of a door or arch to give an appearance of solidity.

Set-up   The actual setting up of the scenery on the stage.

Setting-line   Line drawn on the ground-plan from the PS return to the OP return and marking the fourth wall of the set, ie showing the line downstage of which no scenery is set.

Sight lines   The lines marking off the maximum and minimum areas of the stage that are visible to the audience.

Sill   All doors and arches have an iron sill which runs along the floor to give strength and support between the two uprights.

Size   Glue in powder or jelly form.

Spray gun   Employed to spray a fine coat of paint on the scenery.

Stage cloth   A tough canvas floor cloth, covering the main part of the stage and usually extending in width and depth to the actual setting surrounding the acting area. It can be painted with scene paint or aniline dyes can be used. If the stage floor is visible to all or part of the audience, then its painting should be an intrinsic part of the scenic design.

Stiles   The vertical wooden framework of a flat.

Tabs   Curtains.

Traverse tabs   Curtains hanging upstage of the main curtains, and which can be closed to conceal the upstage area, perhaps while scenery is being changed.

Trucks   See boat trucks.

Unit set   Settings in which the main features of the scenery remain unchanged throughout the play, and to which are added various units to indicate changes of scene.

Vision scene   A device in which gauze is fixed and tightly stretched over an opening and then painted so that it looks solid when lit up from the front, but which becomes transparent when lit up from behind.

Vista scene   A device in which receding wing-pieces are erected, one behind the other and on both sides of the stage. The space on stage centre, between the pair of pieces, decreases the farther away one gets from the proscenium, thus creating an illusion of vista or distance.

References

1   Jean-Louis Barrault, essay on *Total Theatre* in *Theatre Quarterly*, April 1973

2   Edward Gordon Craig, *The Art of the Theatre*, Foulis London, 1905

3   Peter Brook, *The Empty Space*, Penguin Harmondsworth, 1972

4   Edward Gordon Craig, *The Theatre Advancing*, Constable London, 1921

5   *The Drama Review*, New York University School of Arts, June 1973

6   See Suzanne Langer *Philosophical Sketches*, John Hopkins Press New York, 1962, for a study of the objective and subjective in art

7   Antonin Artaud, *The Theatre and its Double* translated by Victor

Corti and published by Calder and Boyars London, 1970
8   Ibid
9   Ibid
10 Ibid
11 Ibid. Brecht's adaptations include versions of Gay's *The Beggar's Opera* and Farquhar's *The Recruiting Sergeant*. Grotowski has created his own scenarios based on a great range of famous texts. See *Theatre Quarterly*, April 1973
12 From an article in *Theatre Quarterly*, January 1973
13 Ibid
14 Bernard Shaw, *Advice to a Young Critic*, Owen London, 1956
15 Peter McKeller, *Imagination and Thinking*, Cohen and West London, 1957
16 Suzanne Langer, *Philosophical Sketches*, John Hopkins Press New York, 1962
17 T Komisarjevsky, *The Theatre*, Bodley Head London, 1935
18 From *Acting in the Sixties*, edited by Hal Burton and published by the BBC London, 1970
19 Bertolt Brecht, *The Messingkauf Dialogues*, Methuen London, 1965
20 T Komisarjevsky *Myself and the Theatre*, Heinemann Educational London, 1929
21 From an interview with Ronald Hayman, *The Times*, 2nd June 1973
22 See especially J L Moreno, *Who Shall Survive?*, Beacon House New York, 1934. Also *The Theatre of Spontaneity*, Beacon House New York, 1949
23 John Dexter, interviewed by Ronald Hayman, *The Times*, 28th July 1973
24 From an article by I M Zanotto in *The Drama Review*, New York University School of Arts, June 1973
25 For a full-scale indictment of the multi-purpose hall, there is an excellent monograph entitled *College Drama Space*, edited by Richard Courtney, written for the University of London Institute of Education, 1964
26 From a review of a production of *Dandy Dick* in *The Times*, 26th July 1973
27 See the article by Peter Moro on theatres and stages in Stirling University's journal *Architectural Design*, Number 3, 1973

Reading List

On the idea of a production
Eric Bentley, *The Life of the Drama*, Methuen London, 1965
Peter Brook, *The Empty Space*, Penguin Harmondsworth, 1972
Raymond Williams, *Drama in Performance*, Penguin Harmondsworth, 1968

On directing
Toby Cole and Helen Chinoy, *Directors on Directing*, Owen London, 1964
John Gielgud, *Stage Directions*, Heinemann London, 1963
Alfred Rossi, *Minneapolis Rehearsals — Tyrone Guthrie Directs Hamlet*, University of California, 1970
Bernard Dukore, *Bernard Shaw, Director*, George Allen and Unwin London, 1971

On acting
Toby Cole and Helen Chinoy, *Actors on Acting*, Crown New York, 1949
Ronald Hayman, *Techniques of Acting*, Methuen London, 1969
Athene Seyler and Stephen Haggard, *The Craft of Comedy*, Muller London, 1943
C Stanislavsky, *An Actor Prepares*, Penguin Harmondsworth, 1967

On designs and staging
Rene Hainaux, *Stage Design Since 1960*, Harrap London, 1973
Stephen Joseph (editor), *Actor and Architect*, Manchester University, 1964
Kenneth Rowell, *Stage Design*, Studio Vista London, 1969
Michael Warre, *Designing and Making Stage Scenery*, Studio Vista London, 1966

On lighting
Frederick Bentham, *The Art of Stage Lighting*, Pitman London, 1970
Richard Pilbrow, *Stage Lighting*, Studio Vista London, 1970
Rank Strand Electric's magazine *Tabs* is very useful, as also are the occasional lectures which they organise. Contact *Tabs* at 29 King Street, Covent Garden, London WC2

On Laban's theory of movement
Rudolf Laban, *The Mastery of Movement*, Macdonald and Evans London, 1960

On improvisation
Theatre Quarterly, January 1973, article by David Clegg, also the following issue with the correspondence following Clegg's article

On stage management
Hal D Stewart, *Stage Management*, Pitman London, 1957

On costume design and making

Motley, *Designing and Making Stage Costumes*, Studio Vista London, 1970

Mary Fernald and Eileen Shenton, *Costume Design and Making*, Black London, 1937

On stage make-up

T W Bamford, *Practical Make-up for the Stage*, Pitman London, 1952

Eric Jones, *Stage Make-up for the School Play*, Batsford London, 1969

On teaching drama

Gerald Gould, *Dramatic Involvement*, Blackwell Oxford, 1970.

Joan Haggerty, *Please, Miss, Can I Play God?* Methuen London, 1966

John Hodgson, editor, *The Uses of Drama*, Methuen London, 1972

John Hodgson and Ernest Richards, *Improvisation*, Methuen London, 1967

Colin King, *A Space on the Floor*, Ward Lock London, 1972.

David Male, *Approaches to Drama*, Unwin London, 1973

William Martin and Gordon Vallins, *Exploration Drama*, Evans London, 1968

R N Pemberton-Billing and J D Clegg, *Teaching Drama*, University of London, 1968

Peter Slade, *An Introduction to Child Drama*, University of London, 1969

Stanislavski, *C. Stanislavski on the Art of the Stage*, Faber London, 1967

Rex Walford and J L Taylor, *Simulation in the Classroom*, Penguin Harmondsworth, 1972

Brenda Walker, *Teaching Creative Drama*, Batsford London, 1970

Brian Way, *Development Through Drama*, Longman London, 1967

For Theatrical Suppliers of all kinds of props, costumes, furniture, lighting, etc, the most reliable way for securing an up-to-date list is by purchasing a copy of *Contacts* from Spotlight, 42 Cranbourn Street, London WC2

Index